Flatwork
Foundation for Agility

By Barb Levenson

Publishing

Flatwork
Foundation for Agility
Barbara Levenson

Dogwise Publishing
A Division of Direct Book Service, Inc.
403 South Mission Street, Wenatchee, Washington 98801
1-509-663-9115, 1-800-776-2665
www.dogwisepublishing.com / info@dogwisepublishing.com

Edited by Nini Bloch, Monica Percival, Marcille Ripperton, and Lisa Baird
Book design and typesetting by Marianne Harris
Cover photo by Lesley Mattuchio, www.pbase.com/lesleylou

Limits of Liability and Disclaimer of Warranty:
The author and publisher shall not be liable in the event of incidental or consequential damages in connection with, or arising out of, the furnishing, performance, or use of the instructions and suggestions contained in this book.

All photographs, except where otherwise noted, are by Cindy Noland, www.nolanddogart.com

Trademarks: All service marks, trademarks, and product names used in this publication belong to their respective holders.

First edition 2007
Reprinted 2010, 2018

ISBN 978-1-61781-235-4

Dedication

This book is dedicated to my students—past, present, and future.

My students are primarily "pet-dog" people, those who have discovered agility after completing a basic obedience course. The majority of them enjoy the camaraderie with friends and the relationship they develop with their dogs. They don't strive to be on a world team; they just want to have fun playing with their dogs. This little book came out of addressing my students' needs for control, focus, and connection with their dogs on course. Teaching these behaviors to dogs without obstacles, I found, worked best. It is to these students that I dedicate this book.

Table of Contents

About the Author

When Barb Levenson took her young German Shepherd, Misty, to a local obedience class in Dallas, she did not realize that her instructors had earned multiple obedience championships with their dogs. They introduced her to the world of competitive obedience and recognized and nurtured both Barb's and Misty's potential. Barb and her German Shepherd went on to win their classes and earn a CD just as the dog turned one year of age.

Finding that she enjoyed training and teaching, Barb combined the two when she returned to Pittsburgh in 1983 and began teaching obedience privately to people in her community. But she was uncomfortable with the compulsion method popular among trainers in the mid-'80s and early '90s. She saw her own Border Collie T.D. developing more and more avoidance behaviors in the ring. At one obedience trial T.D. wouldn't bring the dumbbell to Barb; he preferred to take it to the judge. This behavior spoke volumes to Barb. She realized that many of the problems facing obedience dogs were a result of the

Photo Credit: Bill Weismann

improper use of compulsion. Listening to her own dogs, Barb began to look for other methods. Influenced by Ted Turner (from Sea World), Leslie Nelson, Patti Ruzzo, and others, Barb began introducing positive reinforcement methods into her teaching and training as early as 1989. Recent influences include Nancy Gyes, Tracy Sklenar and Susan Garrett. By the time she opened her own training school in 1991,

Barb with Fly and Class.

she was using positive reinforcement in her puppy, basic obedience, and Canine Good Citizen classes and, shortly after, in her competition obedience classes.

Barb added the sport of agility to her school in 2000 and a couple of years later began teaching the classes herself. Barb's approach to both agility and obedience has her marching to a different drummer, in part shaped by her equestrian experience. She believes that the best way to develop handling skills is "on the flat"—away from the equipment—and incorporates ideas from the horse world about training dogs on the flat. Barb also believes that a strong foundation in obedience sets the stage for a solid relationship with the dog that is critical to enjoying and succeeding in agility. And that means training and refining the communication—especially body language—between dog and handler. To date she has competed with 11 dogs and has titles in obedience (Canadian and American), agility, and herding, rally and tricks.

Introduction: Flatwork or Heelwork for Agility

I first learned about the concept of flatwork when I attended Susan Garrett's Say Yes Puppy Camp three years ago. There I learned about the importance of teaching my young dog how to follow my body without the distraction and interference of obstacles. We practiced many of the skills we would need on course—same-side turns, front crosses, and the beginning of rear crosses. Learning to communicate with a dog through flatwork made a huge impression on me. I realized both its importance and the fact that I had not taught it to my first two agility dogs.

I began using the term flatwork for these exercises because I come from an equestrian background. Young jumpers spend a great deal of time on the flat learning "obedience" to the rider's aides, such as rein and leg signals. And since I also come from a strong competition obedience background in the dog world, it was easy for me to make the paradigm leap.

Photo Credit: Bill Weismann

A horse learns to respond to rein and leg pressure so that his rider can change pace and direction. Here leg pressure on the horse's left side aids in turning him right.

Like me, most people starting out in agility prefer to practice obstacles and sequences because it seems to be so much fun for the dogs. In agility, however, your dog actually spends more time on the flat running with you to the obstacles than he does performing the obstacles. Thus, what happens *between* the obstacles is at least as important as what happens *on* the obstacles. It's on the flat, after all, that you set your dog up for the next obstacle or sequence. It's on the flat where you as handler do most of your job guiding the dog. Performing flatwork successfully requires excellent communication between dog and handler.

To run agility successfully with your dog, you need to develop a clear, coherent, and timely communication system that relies more on body language than words. The pick-up signal cues a change of direction.

Practicing your signals without your dog helps you become a better handler. Practicing signals with your dog but without the equipment—flatwork—fine-tunes the system. At right, a dog targets Levenson's hand from a distance. Targeting forms the basis for training the pick-up signal at the far left.

What do I mean by communication? Did you ever have to "walk through your dog" when he was in the way in the kitchen while you were putting away groceries? Your stepping toward him made him move because dogs respond to social pressure just as we humans do. Dogs and humans have a personal space. You may have experienced this when speaking to someone who steps in too close to you. Automatically you will move back, yielding to their social pressure.

I use the term social pressure when referring to using our bodies to push the dog into a different line or move toward and or away from us. In agility, we frequently use social pressure to change our dogs line toward, or away from, a different obstacle.

It's no wonder that dogs are exquisite readers of body language—but we humans are often woefully unaware of what we are "saying" to our canine partners. Our pace, direction, body position, and movement of head, feet, shoulders, hands, even fingers all communicate volumes to our dogs. Much of learning agility handling is learning to make all our body language clear, consistent, and coherent and to give timely cues.

The need for excellent communication is what I began to understand when I attended Susan's puppy camp. Since then, I've learned that most of the top agility trainers incorporate some kind of pre-obstacle training on the flat into the early schooling of their dogs. Flatwork essentially teaches the dog agility movements without any obstacles. But it does much more: It develops and hones a communication system with your dog. That's because practicing flatwork requires that you become aware of what your body is saying to your dog. You must develop a set of cues and movements that will indicate specific behaviors to the dog. And before you ever bring a dog into the picture, you should be absolutely clear about the movements and how to execute them. Flatwork is your foundation in agility because it teaches you how to handle and it teaches your dog how to stay with you on course.

Because I have a over 30 years training competition obedience dogs, I like to describe agility as *obedience on the fly*. And in my mind it makes sense to treat it as such. I even sometimes refer to flatwork as "heelwork" because it so closely resembles how I teach my competition obedience dogs to follow cues for left and right turns, for changes of pace, and so on. A clever handler can teach a dog most of the movements for agility without the distraction and interference of the obstacles. Additionally, flatwork can help an obstacle-focused dog become more balanced by bringing his attention back to the handler at critical points when it needs to be there.

The basic elements of flatwork are:

- *Straight-line* heeling helps the dog learn to execute a straight line of obstacles on the course

- *Large circles* help the dog learn lateral distance work and negotiating long, rounded distances between obstacles

- *Small circles and figure eights* teach the dog to follow the handler in tight sequences, such as 180's, 270's, advanced courses

- *Serpentines* teach the dog the changes of pace and direction in tight quarters that are required for advanced courses

- *Front and rear crosses* train the dog to negotiate side, direction, and lead changes necessary on course

The more you practice the skills outlined in *Flatwork: Foundation for Agility*, the more fluent your dog will become—and the more proficient your dog will actually be on course. Properly trained, flatwork is anything but dull; it becomes a great dance or game of chase for your dog. Have fun!

Chapter 1: Before You Start

The objective of *Flatwork: Foundation for Agility* is to teach your dog most of the movements he will see in agility without the distraction of any obstacles. The first requirement is that the handler must be clear about the nature of flatwork: the dog's focus on the handler; the movement and position of the handler's body, hands, head, shoulders, and feet when teaching the dog; and the pace the exercise requires. Before you start, you should consider these elements as well as the mechanics and method of reinforcing your dog.

The Dog's Position

One of the first things to consider is the dog's position relative to the handler's body, *a default position* just as the one competition obedience trainers use. That position should be as near to "heel position" as possible—and taken on both the right and left sides of the handler. The American Kennel Club defines heel position as follows: "The dog should be straight in line with the direction in which the handler is facing, at the handler's left side. The area from the dog's head to shoulder is to be in line with the handler's left hip. The dog should be close but not crowding so that the handler has freedom of motion at all times."

Starting out with "heel position" as your default position offers many benefits. It keeps the dog headed in the same direction as you and sets the stage for clear communication when running because you can both see each other when traveling at speed. Also, keeping and reinforcing the dog in heel position prevents you from reinforcing at arbitrary locations, for instance, in "front" position. Reinforcing in front position encourages the dog to continually come around to the front of your body. You do not want your dog defaulting to your front; you'll run into him. You want to teach him (for now) to stay by your side no matter what your pace. Using a position at your heel, either on your right or left side, makes everything clear, concise, and consistent. There is nothing arbitrary about where the dog should be and where you should reinforce him. For agility it is necessary to teach the dog to run on both the handlers' right as well as her left side, but consider the AKC definition. Doesn't it work for agility too? I believe it is an excellent starting position.

Because agility is such a fast-paced sport that depends on quick, accurate communication from the handler to the dog, it makes sense for the dog's default position to be at the handler's side, in line with the handler's body and the direction the handler is heading, as in the left and middle images. Unlike formal obedience, the handler can direct the dog on either side of her body. This default "heel" position allows the dog to see—and respond to—the handler's signals instantly. A dog with his rear angled out, as in the right-hand image, is not in an ideal position to react to his handler's signals.

The Dog's Focus

In agility a dog must be able to focus on both the handler and on the obstacles and to switch back and forth between them when asked to do so. In like fashion, the handler must be able to focus on both his dog and the course, discussed in "Head and Shoulders," page 16. Stuart and Pati Mah refer to the dog's two types of focus as City Driving versus Highway Driving. Some call it handler focus versus obstacle focus. A dog is engaged in highway driving or obstacle focus when he is focused on the obstacle(s) ahead, eager and willing to take that obstacle or series of obstacles. A dog is engaged in city driving or handler focus when his attention is on his handler and he awaits the handler's cues before taking an obstacle. Exclusive focus on the handler or on the obstacles, or the inability to switch between the two, causes problems. A handler-obsessed dog is also sometimes called a "Velcro dog" because he is completely focused on and always runs next to or even slightly behind his handler, rarely taking the initiative to go to an obstacle without his handler's signal. A dog that is solely obstacle focused will run his own course; his handler is superfluous to the exercise.

Agility handlers strive for a balance between handler and obstacle focus and an easy transition between the two. So it stands to reason that the handler must have a clear set of cues to tell the dog when it is okay to go on ahead and when he needs to bring his focus back onto the handler and work closer to his partner. During the dog's foundation training the handler should be teaching obstacles independently of flatwork. By definition, flatwork creates a handler-focused dog. Balancing that flatwork with obstacle training enables the handler to move on to sequencing as a natural outgrowth of the flatwork that has given the dog a set of cues he can understand and rely on.

Obstacle Focus versus Handler Focus: The first time through this rear-cross sequence, the dog at left is so focused on the line of three jumps that he completely misses Levenson's rear-cross signal. The second time through, the dog focuses on Levenson's body language and successfully makes the turn.

Handler Body Movement and Body Position

The position or *change in position* of the handler's head, shoulders, hands, upper body, and feet can cue and create a change in the dog's path or pace. For example, turning the head, shoulders, and body to the right can produce a right turn or an *about turn* (a complete 180° turn to the right). Teaching the dog cues for a left turn requires additional skills if the dog is to maintain heel position on your left side. I'll give details for training the turn in a later chapter. For now it is enough to realize that teaching your dog to take cues from body positions and movements helps to make an agility run smoother and more efficient.

Upper Body

Movement and change in the position of your upper body become an important source of information for your dog. They cue pace and pace changes as well as the direction of travel on the course.

The positions I use to signal pace and pace changes to my dogs are

- *Upright*—cues the dog to go at a normal, brisk, cantering pace.

- *Leaning slightly backward (behind the vertical)*—signals the dog to slow down and shift his focus to the handler. You can also use it to indicate an upcoming tight turn or a down contact so that the dog does not drive ahead.

- *Leaning forward (ahead of the vertical)*—tells the dog he can shift into a fast, obstacle-focused gear for straightaways or in sequences with soft turns where the dog can move at speed away from or with the handler.

Your upper body communicates pace and direction changes. At a normal, fast walk as in the image on the left, a line from your shoulder to your hip should be vertical, signaling to your dog to maintain the same pace. If your upper body shifts back from the vertical, as in the middle image, it cues the dog to put on the brakes, slow down, and focus on you. If you shift your upper body forward from the vertical as in the right-hand image, you're cueing your dog to accelerate and switch his focus to the obstacles ahead.

Head and Shoulders

If a shift in the overall position of your upper body communicates acceleration or deceleration to your dog, turning your head and shoulders can provide a powerful cue for a change of direction. That means your head and shoulders should always be facing in the direction you want the dog to go, and it is critical that you never take your eyes off your dog. Keeping your eyes on your dog means you should also keep your peripheral vision on the course. Therefore it is important to practice running courses without your dog to condition your mind and body to run while watching your dog's path and your path. One of the fastest ways to lose your dog is to look away or elsewhere on the course. This is one of the reasons handlers incur refusals or off-courses.

Several years ago, I attended a Patricia McConnell seminar in which she discussed a little-known fact about dogs. If you look off to the right as though focusing on something interesting, your dog will look in the same direction. I tried this experiment at home with my own dogs. Sure enough, McConnell was right. If you turn your head and look somewhere else on the course (as opposed to where the course is going) the dog most probably will look and then go in that direction, often earning refusals or off-course penalties.

Keep your head and shoulders facing in the direction you want to go, and your dog will follow

Keeping your eyes on both the dog and the course at first seems difficult. In heeling for obedience, however, we learn to watch both the dog and where we are going by using our peripheral vision and also looking straight ahead. Here's an exercise you can use to learn or strengthen this skill.

Stand up straight and put your left hand at the side seam of your pants with your fingers pointing straight ahead. Turn your head very slightly to the left so you can see your fingers wiggle and you can also see objects to the left in your peripheral vision. Take a walk. Can you still focus ahead and peripherally? Jog a bit. Practice this skill with some jumps or obstacles. Now try the same exercise with your right hand. See: you can do it. You can watch your dog and still see where you are going.

With a little practice, you can learn to watch your fingers pointing straight ahead at your pants' seam even with your head focused forward. That means you can both watch the course ahead and the dog at your side.

Feet

Another reason that dogs go off course can be attributed directly to where your feet are pointing. Several months ago I ran a course with my dog Pippin that required her to make a turn to the left after a jump. I was somewhat out of position and my feet were pointing to the right. Even though Pippin was ahead of me, I am convinced she *felt* the direction my feet were pointing. She took the jump to the right, incurring an off-course fault. The video confirmed my suspicions. *Your feet must point in the direction you want the dog to go.*

One more thought about your feet. Dogs have wide peripheral vision and can see your body even when you are behind their position. Keep this in mind when working with your dog.

When a dog can't see your shoulders and head, as when he's coming out of a tunnel, he'll zero in on the direction your feet are pointing to figure out which direction to head in. That means you always need to make sure your feet are pointing where you want your dog to go.

Hands

Your hands—as extensions of your arms—provide vital information to your dog. They direct the dog on course primarily by showing him the path. You can think of a hand signal as a laser pointer used to draw and show the path to the dog. Therefore as a directional signal, the paintbrush should be *ahead* of the dog to indicate the intended path. This takes some practice. Many beginner handlers tend to point at the dog instead of at the upcoming path. Remember, the dog already knows where he is, but only you know where he is going.

Here are a few hand signals that you might consider when training your dog. Keep in mind that most handlers develop their own variations to suit their handling style. Note that the laser pointer cue is a continuous—almost a default—signal whereas the other hand cues are discrete signals requiring a definitive movement of the hand, held for as long as it takes the dog to respond. Most handlers use the hand nearest the dog for cueing him.

Holding the arm and hand nearest the dog in a relaxed L-shape allows your hand to move freely, so it acts like a paintbrush, drawing the path for the dog. Make sure to keep your near hand ahead of the dog, as in the image at right.

On a lead-out, the handler's left hand draws the path for the dog over the jump in line with the direction the handler's feet are going.

- *Follow This Line* — When your dog is traveling close to your path, keep the arm nearest the dog relaxed in somewhat of an L-shape next to your side as your indicator (or lead) hand that draws the path for the dog. For lead-outs, you can use your hand and finger to create a line from the dog's eyes through the line you want him to run.

- *Get Out* (and stay out) — You direct this signal laterally toward the dog's body as though you wanted to try to push the dog away from you. It requires real movement of your arm and hand. Many handlers run with a stiff-armed position that does not allow the handler to push the dog out laterally or to keep the dog on a lateral course necessary for distance work. Since your hand and arm should be able to influence the dog's position relative to the handler—and hence to the course—it pays to keep your arm relaxed until you need to push. Eventually you will be able tell you dog to *Get Out* 20' and if there's a jump, you can direct him to take it, but the initial *Get Out* simply pushes him away from your side.

- *Come In* — Of course, the reverse of the *Get Out* signal is the *Come In* (to me) signal. For this signal you drop your lead hand closer to your body depending on how close you want the dog. Many times on course a handler may want the dog to actually come in to heel position, for instance, to negotiate a tight sequence.

- *Go On* (and take that obstacle) — Many dogs need to be given permission to run ahead of you. To signal your dog to take the obstacle(s) ahead of him push your hand in front of your body, palm facing the intended obstacle.

- *The Pick-Up Cue* — If you need to quickly grab your dog's attention, for instance, if he's just come out of a curved tunnel or if he needs to collect stride for a sharp turn, you can use a quick, definitive flick of the stiff, outstretched index finger of the hand closest to him to cue him to focus on you. Your index finger should point where want your dog to focus and hold position until you get your dog's attention. It also often helps to make eye contact. This pick-up cue is particularly helpful for redirecting the attention of high-drive, obstacle-focused dogs back to the handler.

The *Pick-up* cue is meant to catch the dog's focus and alert him to an upcoming change of path. The handler's relaxed "laser pointer" hand and index finger (left) stiffen (right). Often the handler flicks the hand to flag the dog's attention, as when he is exiting a tunnel and he needs to change direction.

- *The Send* — If your dog is at your side and you want him to take an obstacle ahead of him while you move elsewhere, you can "send" him to the obstacle. The signal resembles the classic bowling motion, starting at your side with the palm up and sweeping more forward than up. You can give your dog more information if, at the same time, you step forward on the same-side foot.

Like a bowling motion, the *Send* signal starts palm up at your side and sweeps forward. It directs your dog to take an obstacle ahead of him.

Hold the signal to show the path. Years ago, I was training my dogs for the Directed Jumping exercise in AKC Utility obedience. In this exercise the handler stands 40' away from the dog and signals a jump by indicating or pointing to a jump. My coaches told me to "hold" the signal, especially in the training stages. I find this advice to be even more critical in agility because the dog is moving so quickly he may not notice the signal. In agility, unlike obedience, the handler can hold the signal for as long as needed until the dog commits to the obstacle. Many people quickly "flip" the signal to the dog. This may be okay for the advanced dog that has learned to read his handler, but the beginner dog has not yet developed the skill to read his handler so readily. Don't flip signals at your dog. Put your hand out and give him enough time to see and process the cue. To improve your hand signals, practice running courses without your dog, keeping your lead hand out at all times and using it clearly to indicate changes of direction.

Unlike in formal obedience competition, in agility you can "hold" the signal as long as it takes for your dog to process it and commit to the next obstacle. This sort of support is especially helpful for beginner dogs.

Thoughts on Reinforcement

Luring versus Reinforcing

Reinforcement is critical if your dog is to learn new behaviors. Training using reinforcement is neither *luring* nor *bribing*. There are distinct differences.

Luring is used to quickly "create" a new behavior and to develop some muscle memory. You can create many behaviors by having the dog follow *a lure,* a piece of food in your hand that is given to the dog upon completion of the behavior. For example, I use a piece of food at a puppy's nose to teach him to sit.

The difficulty with luring is that many people continue to lure the dog well past the point where it is useful. Because the dog is performing the behavior, the handler often believes that his dog understands the behavior, but the dog does not. He is simply following the infamous "carrot" without thinking or learning. His focus is on the food—not on the behavior. Removing the lure early in the learning process will ensure that the dog first learns the behavior and then can reliably perform the behavior without the presence of food in your hand. Scientists and trainers have proven time and time again that dogs *do not learn when they are lured.* At best, they can acquire muscle memory and an elementary understanding of what to do. The handler must then fade the lure and put the behavior on a reinforcement schedule.

Reinforcing, on the other hand, requires the dog to perform a behavior in *anticipation* of getting something he wants, for example a piece of food or a toy. In her book, *Smart Trainers: Brilliant Dogs,* Janet Lewis makes this distinction: "If food (or other appealing stimulus) is to be effective, you must move from using it as a lure to using it as reinforcement. The dog will still be working for the food, but food need not be present for the behavior to occur. Simply stated, the food is presented after the behavior rather than before." Janet suggests that a trainer should get all food off her body as soon as possible. She carries food in plastic bags in her training bag. In the beginning, her bag is always close to where she is training. When the dog gives her a behavior she wants to reinforce, she *marks*[1] the behavior and runs to the training bag. Of course, this regimen is a little harder than keeping food in your pocket or a bait bag, but food in the pocket presents a completely different picture than the dog will ultimately see in competition. It is a costly mistake to teach your dog that you cannot reinforce him unless there is food on your body.

I also believe the dog knows when I have food on my body and when I don't. I have observed my students who are reluctant to wean their dog off the food on their body. When they get around to it during the final week of class, the dog knows that the food is not available and, more often than not, he won't work for the handler. Chris Bach, developer of *The Third Way* method of dog training, believes that the presence of the food (yes, even on your body) actually becomes the cue for the behavior to occur. No food: no behavior. It's as simple as that. So even in this case, the dog is still being lured by the presence of food and is not truly working or offering a behavior in order to earn reinforcement.

Dogs that understand the concept of working to gain reinforcement are defined as being operant. Operant dogs have learned a very powerful concept: *their behavior* earns them food. These dogs are therefore quite willing to offer and quickly learn new behaviors to gain reinforcement. This powerful tool enables a clever trainer to teach a dog virtually anything.

A Cute Luring Story

Kathy, a student and a former instructor, was planning to take over classes at one of my locations. In the six-month transition period she traveled behind me in her car through many back roads to get to the building. When it was time for Kathy to go by herself, she had no idea how to go. Why not? Kathy had been only following the back of my truck. She did not notice the road signs along the way and had not learned the route to the building. She had been traveling behind me for six months, but she was "lured" by my taillights and as a result did not know how to get there on her own. I use this example in classes because it accurately demonstrates how truly ineffective luring can be.

---

[1] *A marker is a word ("Yes", "Good"), a sound (click), or other signal that indicates to the dog that he has performed the correct behavior and will now get reinforced.*

One last note about food: According to Chris Bach, the improper use of food can create a number of potential problems for trainers beyond the dog's reliance on food as a cue for the behavior. Additionally, the handler sees a loss of attitude without the food; and more often than not, the dog is actually unable to perform behaviors when there is no food on the person's body. Finally, and perhaps most notably, the dog cannot proceed successfully to a higher level of training.

By the way, food is not the only reinforcer you can use with your dog. Many dogs would rather get a fetch or tug toy. In the case of flatwork, however, I prefer to use food as a reinforcer because it allows the handler to place the reinforcement in strategic positions and keep the dog in that particular position.

Dogs gravitate to the spot where they receive reinforcement. That means that if you consistently reward your dog with your near hand down your pants' seam, he's more likely to stay in his default heel position.

Where You Reinforce Your Dog Matters

Few people realize how important the placement of reinforcement, especially food reinforcement, is for success in the sport of agility. Top competition obedience trainers have known for years, however, that the placement of their reinforcement affects where the dog gravitates toward. In obedience, if you reinforce heeling straight down your left pants' seam, the dog will be more inclined to stay in heel position. If you consistently reinforce in the center of your body when teaching the dog to come into front position, the dog will learn to find this position more easily. Consistency is crucial.

I can usually tell where my students are reinforcing their dogs. I joke with them that I am the "dog psychic" and that their dogs mentally (telepathically) tell me where they have been reinforced. But it is the *place where the dog goes* that is usually the spot where the handler has been reinforcing. Dogs are drawn toward reinforcement. If they could talk, they would say, "Don't go to Georgia if the gold's in California." Often a novice handler reinforces heeling in front of her body, so the dog begins to rotate progressively toward that front position to get closer to the food. Why is the location of reinforcement important for agility you might ask? If the handler reinforces correctly, down the left or right seam of her pants with the hand close to or touching her body, the dog will find and remain close to this position for flatwork and thus maintain the correct position.

A handler who rewards her dog when he's ahead of her (left-hand image) will encourage forging and possibly crossing in front of her. A handler who treats her dog when he's behind her (right-hand image) will reward lagging and possibly crossing behind her when she can't see her dog. In both cases in an agility setting, the dog could take an off-course.

Reinforcing with the "off" hand (on the other side from the one the dog is on) encourages the dog to bend around in front of the handler as at left, or even face the handler, blocking her path as at right. All these incorrect reinforcement practices can confuse the dog and make it harder for him to learn the default heel position.

Reinforce Where You Want the Dog to Be

Sounds simple, doesn't it? Simply reinforce where you would like your dog—and his focus—to be. Easier said than done because the handler must be clear ahead of time about exactly *where* she wants the dog to be. Consider a couple of different scenarios.

In flatwork for agility, you want the dog on either side of you, in a straight line parallel with your body, neither lagging behind nor forging ahead. You also want the dog paying attention to you. So it stands to reason that where you place your reinforcer will have an impact on the resulting behavior. I recommend reinforcing down the seam of your pants and slightly above the dog's nose. Be sure to reinforce the dog only when he is aligned straight next to your body. Similarly, when I teach weave poles to a young dog, I deliver my reinforcement by throwing it straight at the end of the poles. This keeps the dogs head straight and motivates driving straight through and out of the poles.

Be careful where you reward your dog for a two-on/two-off performance of the A-frame contact. Reinforcing with the near hand keeping the dog's head straight, as in the left-hand image, will give you a dog that's more likely to look ahead on course. Using the off-side hand to reward your dog, as in the right-hand image, causes your dog to turn his head and focus on you.

The point is that you must think ahead about the placement of your reinforcement. It's not enough just to be a Pez dispenser that doles out food to the dog. It is vital to deliver it in the correct position so that you are reinforcing where you want the dog to focus and ultimately to be.

Did you know? Pants have seams to help obedience and agility people reinforce correctly.

Stop to Reinforce Behaviors

When training flatwork I believe it is essential to be clear to the dog about the exact behavior you are reinforcing, so I stop my forward motion immediately when I see the behavior I want to reinforce. As I stop I mark that particular behavior with either a click or the word "Yes" and then reinforce down the seam of my pants with the hand closest to the dog. I believe stopping, marking, and reinforcing in this way puts a "magnifying glass" on the exact behavior and helps the dog know precisely *which* behavior is being reinforced.

I watch beginner students in my classes mark a behavior and continue moving as they reinforce. My question to them is, "How does the dog know which behavior he is being reinforced for?" As an example, think of heeling as individual frames in a moving picture, numbered from 1 to 10. If frame 4 is the behavior you want to reinforce but you keep walking until frame 9 and actually reinforce frame 9, which behavior are you reinforcing? Furthermore, does the dog have any idea what the reinforcement is for? You must "freeze-frame," so to speak, to communicate effectively with your dog. For instance, if you are training a correct position on the down contact of the A-frame, you must stop instantly at the A-frame down contact, mark the behavior, and reinforce the dog in the correct position. Then begin again with another repetition.

Generous Reinforcement Speeds Learning

A dog's learning rate is directly proportional to your rate of reinforcement. The higher the value and the more frequent the reinforcement (especially in the beginning), the faster the dog learns the behavior. Don't be stingy with reinforcement. You can fade it later. Your reinforcement is information to the dog telling him that he is correct. The more the dog understands his behavior is correct the more confident he becomes and the faster he learns. Use a high rate of reinforcement the instant your dog offers the behavior you are looking for. It's your job to give him accurate and instantaneous feedback for his successful efforts.

With these considerations in mind it is now time to start training your agility dog.

Chapter 2: Straight-line Heeling for Agility

When I teach obedience heeling to my young dogs, I always begin by teaching all behaviors in slow motion so the dog can more easily learn the behaviors. Dogs cannot think as well when they are moving quickly. Speed tends to put them into "drive" and they may become aroused as a result. Aroused dogs are reactive. Reactive dogs are not thinking dogs and consequently they are less likely to learn.

With my beginner, sometimes called "green" dogs, I take as much time as is necessary to explain, through my reinforcement, exactly which specific behaviors I want them to learn. In obedience, I want the dog in heel position with his head up and his eyes focused on me. I want him by my side, neither forging ahead nor lagging behind. Starting slowly, I don't increase speed until the dog is quite clear and sure about the desired position at the slow speed. And in the beginning, I reward frequently and generously, developing a high rate of reinforcement for the behavior I am teaching. Agility flatwork uses the same concept but without the intense eye contact required for today's obedience competition.

Initially, I teach my dogs only straight-line heeling. I want them to be able to travel a *long* straight line before I put in any circles or turns. And so it is for agility flatwork. A major portion of course work is a straight line to a turn. A dog should first learn to travel straight with the handler. I add the circles and turns later.

The classical obedience posture (left) keeps the left hand close to the body and head straight ahead; communication relies more on verbal commands with little eye contact and only subtle body language cues. In agility (middle), the handler typically keeps the hand and arm nearest the dog in a relaxed L-shape, enabling the hand to draw the path for the dog. The dog (right) is in an excellent position to read his handler's body language and cues.

Before You Get Your Dog

Your first day of training this crucial behavior is critical to what happens down the road. You *must be absolutely clear* about your criteria. Before beginning to train, think about the precise behavior you want to see in order to reinforce it. Imprint it clearly in your mind so you will know it when you see it. It would be helpful to stand in front of a mirror and practice walking in a straight line and reinforcing *without* your dog. Make a fist with each hand (you'll be carrying treats in each hand) and carry your arms slightly bent and loose at your sides with the index finger of your indicator hand drawing the dog's path. Can you look at your virtual dog and walk straight ahead at the same time? Practice your walking, then stop, mark, and reinforce your virtual dog. Remember to reinforce exactly where you want the dog to be. I suggest that you develop the habit of reinforcing the dog at your pants' seam. Get these behaviors so clear in your mind that you do not have to think about your job. Then you are free to concentrate on teaching your dog.

For greater precision in indicating the path, it helps to "draw the line" for your dog with your index finger (left), keeping it ahead of the dog. When you first start heeling with your dog, you'll conceal a treat in either fist (right).

Practicing *without* your dog is a key element that is often neglected in the beginning stages of training flatwork for agility. You must be able to perform your footwork, marking, and reinforcing without having to think about or focus on it. If you are thinking about what *you* have to do, how can you be thinking about teaching and reinforcing your dog? You cannot be your dog's teacher when your focus is on your own behavior.

Teaching Straight-line Heeling

With food in both hands and your dog on your left side, begin walking at a slow pace. Use your *lead hand* (the hand next to the dog is considered the "lead" hand), in this case the left hand, to direct the dog to follow you in what approximates heel position. I suggest using a pointed index finger with a closed fist in training so you can keep your food, or a clicker, hidden in your hand. Although you do not need to have the strong attention necessary for competition obedience, you do need the dog's focus on *you*. It is that very focus and the dog's remaining in position beside you that you are actually reinforcing.

Start with a very slow and deliberate pace. At first as you begin to explain this new behavior to your dog, reinforce him for *every correct step*. This reward is critical since your reinforcement teaches your dog to follow your lead hand. Look at and evaluate each step the dog takes as you go along. The behaviors or criteria you want to reinforce are as follows: The dog is by your side with his attention focused on you. He is neither sniffing the ground nor wandering about. His body is straight and parallel to your body and he is not forging ahead or lagging behind you.

For the first two days practice only one step at a time, click or mark, and reinforce. Get the behavior very clear and solid in your dog's mind. Don't be afraid to stay at this point for several days if necessary and don't worry about repetition. I have overheard handlers saying that their dog gets bored with repetition. If, however, you are reinforcing every step and throwing in some praise, it is highly unlikely your dog will get bored with the "game." Instead, he will actually become confident in himself and his ability to be correct.

For normal pace (a walk at a good clip), your upper body should be nearly vertical.

Dogs don't get bored. Their trainers are boring. Think about your dog's favorite game. My dogs love fetch. They would play fetch forever if I let them. Do they get bored? Of course they don't. The game is reinforcing for them. Your training games must be reinforcing.

If your dog becomes bored, look at how you are training. Are you slow with your marker and reinforcement? Do you fumble with the food? Are you uncertain about what you are reinforcing so that the entire game slows to a snail's pace? Moving the game too slowly causes boredom. An analogy that helps my students understand this concept is the RPM speeds utilized years ago for vinyl records. There were three speeds – 33 1/3, 45 and 78 rpm. Obviously 33 1/3 was the slowest speed with 78 as the quickest. I find our dogs want the game to go at 78 rpm. Often, we are stuck at 45 or even 33 1/3. It is natural for them to begin looking for something else to do as we fumble around. That is why practicing without your dog is so important. You must keep the game exciting and moving quickly; otherwise you risk losing your dog's focus and attention.

After you have walked and reinforced 10 to 15 steps with your dog on your left side, turn toward your dog and give him the pick-up cue with your right hand to grab his attention. He should turn toward you and reverse his direction, so now he is traveling on your right side, following your right lead hand. *Note*: I use the term "pick him up on the left/right side" whenever I change lead hands. If I am handling with my dog on the left and change sides, I am careful to pick up the dog—making sure that I have his attention and have refocused him on my "new" lead hand—before continuing in the new direction. Repeat the straight-line heeling exercise on the right side.

To pick up your dog on your right hand, turn left, toward him, giving the pick-up signal with your stiff right hand. He will turn toward you. Keep turning left as he comes into your right hand, and he will end up in heel position on your right side.

Notice the dog's behavior on each side. Is it the same? If your dog has had a lot of obedience training, you will notice he is significantly better at heeling on your left side. If you are starting with a dog that has not been taught to heel, it may actually be a little easier for you. (See "Flatwork: A Microcosm of Agility Problems.") Whichever side is the most difficult to train, train that side 60% to 70% of the time and the other side 30% to 40%. "Train to dog's your weakness" is one of the most important concepts in dog training.

> Train to your dog's weakness

Once your dog is clear and proficient with heeling one step, you can increase the number of steps you require for reinforcement. At this point, let's discuss schedules of reinforcement.

Flatwork: A Microcosm of Agility Problems

On the day I wrote this section, I went to my agility building to work each of my three dogs. I wanted to see where each would fit into this program and what their individual needs might be. It was astounding! By performing this first exercise of straight-line agility heeling with each dog, I saw a microcosm of each dog's problems. The dogs and their problems are:

Pippin, a six-year-old Border Collie that was started as a competition obedience dog:

In my experiment I found she could not move well on my right side. She was fluid and flexible on my left, but on the right she was stiff, swung wide, and arced away from me around toward my front, the exact behavior she does in the ring. I began to see also that she was trying to get around to my front so she could pivot into heel position.

Presto, a three-year-old Australian Shepherd that was started in agility at three months:

Presto could heel on both sides rather fluidly and easily, but he could not rotate his hindquarters on my right side as well as he could on my left. And because his body type is different from that of a Border Collie, his spine was not as supple, making certain moves more difficult for him.

Zippy, My one-year-old Border Collie and my newest agility prospect:

Wouldn't you know it? Zippy was the best of the three. He was equally comfortable on either my right or my left side although he did want to forge a bit on the right. He's been trained in competition obedience heeling so I was not surprised. Unlike the other dogs, he was able to rotate his hindquarters in either direction. This is a result of Susan Garrett's "Perches," a game that teaches puppies and dogs to rotate their hindquarters. (See "Teaching Movement of the Hindquarters" page 39.)

At left the dog is crabbing (front end in correct alignment but rear out) in response to his handler's sudden slowing. At right the dog got too excited about the fast pace and forged ahead of his handler.

Schedules of Reinforcement

There are several types of reinforcement schedules used in training dogs.

- *Continuous Reinforcement Schedules:* In a fixed reinforcement schedule every correct response is reinforced. I use a continuous reinforcement schedule when my dogs are first learning a behavior. A continuous reinforcement schedule would be used for those important first steps in flatwork, reinforcing every step that is *correct*.

- *Fixed Ratio Schedules:* Once the dog understands the initial behavior I change to a fixed ratio schedule in which I reinforce for a specific number of correct responses. I begin to reinforce for every 2 correct responses. When the dog has achieved 8 out of 10 correct responses at that level, I begin reinforcing for 3, then 4, then 5 correct responses, and so on.

- *Fixed Interval Schedules:* In a fixed interval schedule the handler reinforces the dog for maintaining his behavior for a fixed period of time. A fixed interval schedule is used for the beginning stages of sit-stays and lead-outs.

- *Variable Ratio Schedules:* I use a variable schedule of reinforcement in flatwork once the dog has learned to stay with me for at least 7 steps before being reinforced. At this level you begin to vary the number of steps you require before reinforcing thus reinforcing at unpredictable times in the process. This is perhaps the most important schedule for flatwork. In this schedule the dog learns to take more steps because he believes that his next step may earn him reinforcement.

With variable ratio schedules, however, it is quite easy to move too fast. In other words, handlers often require too many steps before reinforcing the dog. If the task seems too hard, the dog may get frustrated and quit trying. When using this type of schedule, remember to help your dog be successful. Decide on an *average* number of steps with a high and a low number of steps and vary within that average. For example using an average of 5 steps, I reinforce for 10 steps, 5 steps, 7, 3, 9, and even 1 step. Once the dog is successful at an average of 5, I increase the average to 10 with 5 steps as the low and 15 as the high level. Every once in a while I even throw in a "surprise" reinforcement for 2 or 3 steps just to keep things unpredictable.

A "variable" ratio schedule does not imply relaxing criteria for reinforcement. If the handler allows the dog to lag, forge, or sniff for a couple of steps of heeling and then reinforces, she will reinforce an incorrect chain of behaviors, confuse the dog, and lengthen the time it takes him to learn the correct behavior. Make sure you maintain strict criteria during this stage of training.

- *Variable Interval Schedules:* In a variable interval schedule the handler varies the amount of time between reinforcements. Variable interval schedules are helpful for teaching sit-stays and down-stays for the table, among other uses. The dog knows he will be reinforced but just never knows quite when.

Note: Behaviors that are on a variable schedule of reinforcement are the strongest behaviors and are more resistant to extinction than continuous schedules. Keep this point in mind and use a continuous schedule for as short a time as possible.

Continue to work straight-line agility heeling for as long as it takes your dog to become proficient and clear about what is expected. Keep on working until your dog can heel in a straight line of 60' to 100' on either side of you without forging, lagging, or *crabbing*.[2] Many people tend to want to rush training straight-line agility heeling and move on before the dog is clear and the behavior is solid. The longer you remain at this step, however, the easier it will be for you in the more advanced stages. You are teaching your dog *where* you want his body to be and *how* to travel in a path parallel to you. This step is crucial and should not be short-changed in any way, because truly it sets the stage for what is to come.

---

[2] *In heeling, crabbing describes a dog whose head is in heel position but whose rear is angled away from you. Crabbing is typically caused either by reinforcing toward the front of your body or by transferring food from your right hand to your left hand in front of your body. The dog sees the food transfer and rotates so he can get to the food more quickly.*

One last note about heeling for agility: In no way does this training interfere with the dog's ability to work at a distance. I consider distance work for agility just another skill to teach my dog, a skill that has its own set of cues and signals just as flatwork does. Flatwork, done correctly, sets your dog up for more advanced work, including distance work, because it lays the foundation for the cues you will use in the future.

Once the dog is able to heel nicely on either side at a normal walking pace, you are ready to add pace variations.

Fast and Slow Pace

In competition obedience, the handler cues her dog for fast and slow pace by changing the position of her upper body as well as the speed and length of her stride. You may not know it but your dog already understands much of this body language naturally. For instance, get up off the sofa and move quickly and deliberately toward your bedroom with your body inclined slightly forward and your eyes looking in the direction you are headed. Your dog most probably will get up and run ahead of you toward the bedroom and perhaps even beat you there. Or get up and creep into another room slowly and uncertainly as your eyes dart around. Your dog will watch you carefully but will not know where to go because you are giving him no deliberate body cues. Understanding and using your dog's ability to read changes in your body position, pace, stride length, and focus will sharpen the communication between you and your canine partner. These body language cues give you a quick, natural signal system to cue the dog to slow down or speed up in anticipation of changes on a course.

Teaching a Fast Pace

Having a dog that will instantly change gears to a fast canter or gallop can save you time on wide-open courses and straightaways. To cue the dog for a fast pace, bend your upper body forward at the waist so you are slightly *in front of the vertical.* Increase both your stride pace and stride length taking *longer* strides so you are covering more ground faster than you do at a normal pace. Your body posture and longer stride length tell the dog, "We're going fast!" To cue the change from fast to normal, straighten your body back to the upright position you used for normal flatwork and return to your "normal" stride length and pace.

To cue a faster pace, lean your upper body forward and increase both the rhythm and length of your strides.

In teaching flatwork to your dog I have found it necessary to *hear* a rhythm in my head. For normal pace I hear a quick 1-2-3-4 in my head. That beat comes from years of heeling to a metronome. If you can find a portable metronome, set it to 135 beats per minute. A fast pace covers more ground both because of the longer stride length and faster pace. When I am performing a *slow* pace, I just add an "and" to the rhythm, 1-and-2-and-3-and, and so on.

Before you try teaching your dog a fast pace, practice speeding up and slowing down by yourself so you are perfectly clear that you can do your job correctly. When you feel you are ready, get your dog and start with your dog on your left side at a normal pace. Use the pointed index finger of your lead hand to draw the path for the dog. Take several steps at a normal pace, then lean your body forward, and shift into your fast pace.

With a somewhat passive dog it may be helpful at first to encourage him with some verbal *Rahs* or even *Let's go!* The word at this point has no meaning to the dog. The purpose in using it is only to elevate the dog's *emotional state*. The word can also alert him that something new is coming and he should pay attention.

Be sure to eliminate the words as soon as possible. It's your *body cue* that you want the dog to notice. In addition, if there are no words attached to the behavior, *you* must alter your body cue and avoid the trap of putting words onto every behavior. Dogs are naturally adept at watching our bodies. Your dog will learn this new movement quickly, but you must give him *immediate* information when he is correct.

Aroused or Reactive Dogs

Some dogs become very aroused with the transition to a fast pace. They may jump and bite if the handler immediately breaks into a run. For these dogs it is best to break this exercise down into smaller steps. Start with a slightly brisker speed than your normal pace and gradually build up to a fast pace. Also reinforce after three to four running steps. This way you are shifting into a faster gear, but the dog doesn't have a lot of time to get aroused. By the time you have reinforced your dog 10 times, he will already be thinking about how to gain reinforcement and will be less likely to become as aroused. Once your dog has learned to pick up his pace on your body cue, you then can gradually increase your pace until you are running.

Reinforcing the Fast Pace

As soon as your dog accomplishes two to three running steps, mark the behavior with a click or "Yes" and throw a couple of pieces of food ahead of you. Here you want to reinforce the dog for speeding up. Therefore, if you slow down to feed the dog at your side and the dog responds, you are reinforcing him for returning to normal pace, which is not your goal. At this point, it is important to reinforce the dog for responding to the fast cue and changing his behavior.

Evaluate each sequence carefully and reinforce only behavior that meets the same criteria you used at your normal pace—the dog should be straight and parallel beside you, without forging, lagging, or crabbing. Take your time at this important stage. Build a strong reinforcement history for the behavior. You are laying the foundation for what is to come.

To reinforce your dog for picking up his pace in response to your cue, it's clearer and more motivating to click and toss food or a toy ahead of him than to stop to feed him at your side.

Practice transitions from normal to fast at first. After the dog is responding immediately to your fast cue on either side of you it is time to become less predictable about how often you reinforce your dog. Becoming more variable early in the training allows you to (slowly) begin fading your complete reliance on food. A variable schedule is also the most resistant to extinction. So instead of reinforcing an exact number of steps, vary the number of steps you take before rewarding your dog. You also can increase the amount of food *(jackpot)* you give at these varying intervals.

Once your dog is reliably speeding up on a variable reward schedule, you can begin speeding up and then cueing your dog to return to normal pace by straightening your body back to the upright position and returning to your regular stride length and pace. Mark and reward his adjusting his pace. Now with the dog on your left, start reinforcing for his adjusting from normal to fast pace several times, then fast to normal, normal to fast, and so on. Again be sure to vary the number of steps so you don't become predictable, and reinforce the dog for responding to the cues. After several repetitions on your left side, switch the dog to your right side by turning toward him and picking him up on your right hand, and repeat on that side. Remember to train your dog more on his weakest side.

When you can run 60' to 100' with your dog on both sides in heel position, with transitional pace changes from normal to fast and back to normal again, you are ready to move on to the slow pace.

Teaching a Slow Pace

The slow-down cue informs the dog to reduce speed and collect his stride for tricky sequences. For example, your dog might be coming out of a fast line of tunnels and jumps when he needs to collect for a sharp turn. I also use this cue on down contacts. I learned this maneuver from Pati Mah, who drives forward fast and hard with her body until the last part of a contact and then shifts her weight backward. In response to the cue, her dogs slow down at the end of the contact. It's a simple cue that also may stop your dog from driving off a contact or running by a weave pole entry. Keep in mind that, for most dogs, teaching them to slow down and collect is harder than teaching them to speed up. Since most dogs like to go fast, it goes against the grain a bit, so be patient with this step.

If leaning forward signals a faster pace, then the cue for a slower pace is just the reverse. I teach my dogs to slow down when my body leans back *behind the vertical.* In addition, I slow the movement of my feet; the stride length remains the same.

Practice the slow pace first without your dog. Begin by walking normally. Then go into a slow pace by leaning back slightly and taking slower steps. Feel the rhythm as you walk. Feel what you are doing with your body. As I

mentioned earlier it is helpful at first to cue your strides with a rhythmic 1-and-2-and-3-and, a technique I learned years ago from an obedience coach. Become conscious and aware of how you are developing your body cue since soon you will be teaching this cue to the dog. When you are sure you understand your job, it's time to get your dog.

Start with your dog on your left at a normal pace. Take several steps and then go into slow-motion mode. Say nothing to the dog but remember to lean back (you may even exaggerate this posture somewhat during the initial training) and slow the rhythm of your steps. Cue yourself silently if you wish. The *instant* you see your dog change his pace and

To cue a slower pace, lean your upper body back and slow the rhythm of your strides. Here the dog has responded to the abrupt change of pace by putting on his own brakes.

slow down, immediately stop, mark, and reinforce the behavior. Then begin again.

Practice normal to slow several times with the dog on the left. Remember that you are reinforcing the dog for recognizing the *transition* to the slow pace. Use your reinforcement to help your dog understand that this shift in your body position has meaning. He will also learn to read your change of pace. He is learning a new behavior so you must tell him the *instant* you see him change his pace. Tell him he is correct by marking and reinforcing just his change of pace at first. There's plenty of time for increased duration once he understands the behavior. When he's responding to your changed posture while he's on your left, turn toward your dog picking him up on your right hand, and repeat with him on the right.

After several repetitions on each side, you should begin to see a noticeable change in your dog's pace as you go from normal to slow. Practice this skill until your dog is changing his pace immediately just by the subtle shift in your body posture. Then begin to add more unpredictability by varying how often you mark and reward and with switches from slow to normal and then to slow again.

Mixing It Up

When you are able to negotiate 100' in a straight line with a switch from normal to slow pace and back again comfortably, challenge your dog with a fun game. Mix up your pace changes on either side. Switch from normal to fast, fast to slow, slow to fast, slow to normal, and so on. Remember to change sides often. Add a lot of variety and unpredictability to this game and keep your rate of reinforcement high. Your dog will love playing this game with you—especially when he is getting reinforced for it.

Chapter 3: Teaching Movement of the Hindquarters

Obedience people have known for years that dogs don't know they have a back end, let alone that they can move it independently of their front end! Much of this awareness among obedience trainers comes from the equestrian world. A horse can cross one hind leg diagonally forward in front of the other hind leg, thus moving the haunches around the forehand in an arc. It's a natural ability that can be trained on command. Equestrians call the ability to rotate the hind legs in a larger circle around the front legs a *turn on the forehand.*

A horse executes the turn on the forehand, rotating his hindquarters to the right. His right hind leg moves to the right. Then he lifts and crosses his left hind leg in front of the right one and moves the right hind leg to the right again. His hindquarters describe an arc around his stationary forequarters.

Why is this behavior necessary for agility dogs? First it gives a handler more control over the shape of circles and tight turns that a dog frequently must negotiate on courses. Since so much of agility is about moving in arcs, teaching your dog to be flexible in the hind end and to move along a curve are critical skills that will pay off handsomely on course. Second, agility dogs should be able to realign with the handler after a turn. Teaching a dog to rotate his hindquarters helps him line up straight with the handler's body and get into heel position—on either side of the handler. Obedience dog trainers call this skill *In* or *Close,* but the name doesn't matter. It's the behavior that's important. Finally, developing rear-end awareness enables a dog to swivel his hips midair over a jump and execute other athletic feats.

A dog executes a turn on the forehand, moving her hindquarters in an arc while her front end pivots in place on the phonebook.

Teaching independent movement of hindquarters can help train a dog to turn tightly after a jump to come into heel position.

While you are teaching your dog to travel with you in a straight line, you can also begin to teach him about the movement of his hindquarters. The basic turn on the forehand behavior is as follows: The dog approaches on the perch or a phonebook, puts his front feet on it and rotates his haunches in an arc left or right depending on the "pressure" the handler applies. *(Author's note: When this book was first published in 2007, phone books were readily available. This is not so now in 2018. Many of my students purchase four or five 12" x 12" tiles and glue them together. It makes a sturdy perch.)*

The Body Language of Pressure

Most animals move *away* from pressure. It's a matter of comfort. Squeezing the sides of a horse with both legs causes the horse to move forward, away from the pressure. A horse learns to move to his right when his rider uses leg pressure on the horse's left side, and vice versa. Most mammals, including humans, prefer that another animal not encroach on their space and try to keep a "comfortable" distance from each other. Especially among social animals, the concept of social distance regulates physical encounters. Animals learn to yield to pressure—from an approaching dog, herd or even a human. Pressure is a universal body language. When your dog is lying down, watch what happens when you start to walk into his "space": *Most* dogs get up and move away. I say "most" dogs because I own a dog that is reluctant to move simply because he is insensitive to any kind of pressure. Teaching this dog to yield to pressure has been and remains a great challenge.

In agility, a dog's responses to pressure, or the lack of it, dictate "working distance"—how far from the handler a dog is comfortable working. If you've ever heard someone say, "I pushed my dog right off that contact," the handler is stating that she got too close (applied too much pressure) to her dog and "forced" him off the contact, away from the handler. Likewise in agility, if you move too far away from your dog, he is likely to come toward you, as many a handler has experienced in attempting a gamble. In teaching a dog to move his hindquarters, your position on either side of your dog and movement toward or away from him can move him right or left. You'll learn to train and use both the push and pull aspects of this essential piece of body language.

The First Step

The first step is to train the dog to put his forepaws on a target and keep them there. Later he can learn to rotate his hindquarters around his front end. You will teach your dog to turn on the forehand *away* from you before you teach him to rotate *toward* you.

I had been teaching the *In* command to my competition obedience dogs for many years, but Susan Garrett's Puppy Camp led the way to a new method of teaching the turn on the forehand that is both as easy as it is fun for the dogs. I first learned about "Perches" when I attended Camp with my young border collie, Zippy. Learning this skill (outlined in *Clean Run Magazine*, March 2003, p.15) enabled Zippy to be much handier about his hindquarters than any other dog I had trained. My previous dogs were only able to perform the hindquarter rotation on my left side.

In my own classes I use phonebooks or perches (see above) for teaching this behavior, small ones for the little dogs and larger ones for big dogs. When using a phonebook, you can tape the book on all three open sides. It will last a long time.

Tools you need to get started:

- A perch or a phonebook

- A clicker if you and your dog are proficient with it. Otherwise the verbal marker, "Yes" will suffice.

- Lots and lots of food.

Shaping a Complex Behavior

There are many steps in acquiring this behavior. If you shape this behavior, which I suggest, you will find that stepping on the book is an "interim" step toward the final behavior. Karen Pryor (*Don't Shoot the Dog!* 1999), the person I credit with bringing clicker training to the dog world, defines shaping as "establishing a series of intermediate goals, and finding some behavior presently occurring to use as a first step." Karen believes the success or failure of shaping does not depend upon expertise as much as persistence. I add one more element to this—a sense of humor. Keep that and you can shape anything.

I suggest using a clicker to mark each behavior and step along the way. The clicker is more precise than your voice and tells the dog the exact behavior you are reinforcing. It is also harder to mark a behavior with a clicker and reinforce *at the same time* than it is to use a verbal marker and simultaneously reinforce, and that's precisely what you want. It is crucial that the clicker be used to *predict* the reinforcement. Often when we use a verbal marker, it is easy to say "Yes" and reinforce with food *at the same time.* The dog is focused on the food and does not *hear* the all-important marker. Learning occurs more slowly if at all.

In the beginning you use the clicker just to get the dog to approach, sniff, and interact with the phonebook. Later you click and treat for lifting a foot, putting a foot on the book, and so on. Although I like and prefer shaping behaviors whenever possible (it's fun both for the dog and for me) it has been referred to as an "untidy progression" because you can't plan what the dog is going to offer you. You

---

Honing Your Clicker Skills

If you are not comfortable using a clicker, stop here and practice some clicker skills. In their book *In Focus,* Deb Jones and Judy Keller describe some great games for handlers to improve their timing skills. Here are a few:

- Throw a tennis ball up in the air and click when it hits the ground.
- Throw the tennis ball up in the air and click when it hits its apex or peak.
- Here's a hard one. Watch a friend and click whenever she blinks.

All these games are designed to improve your ability to "catch" behaviors at the instant they occur. Practicing this skill will help you shape your dog for the phonebook exercise, so practice first before bringing out your dog. Jones also has a great article on shaping in the February 2006 issue of *Clean Run.* It will give you many of the fundamentals of this method that will help you in shaping your dog's behavior.

just have to go with the flow and sometimes reinforce an unexpected behavior that your dog offers because you can see it is leading to the end goal.

Teaching the Perch

Before you actually begin teaching the behavior, here are some important guidelines.

- Do not take your eyes off your dog. You could miss an important opportunity to reinforce behavior.

- Have your clicker and food ready *before* you approach the phonebook. That way you are prepared for any behavior you get, especially if your dog runs right up and steps on the book.

- In the beginning, click for any movement in the direction of the book. When the dog is getting on the book reliably, you can then begin to click for any movement or shuffle of the back end.

- We want the dog to stay focused on task at all times. Sometimes, however, your dog may become distracted, start sniffing away from the perch or even get "stuck." Occasionally when a dog is confused they will default to a known, previously reinforced behavior such as attention or a down. They get stuck in this behavior and stop working or offering behaviors. Given this circumstance I will "reset" the dog. Resets are allowing the dog to leave the situation for a moment and come back. Throw one piece of food away from the perch, tell the dog to "get it" and allow him to return and try again.

  If you try several resets and the dog continues to not be able to work, end this session with a reinforcement of a lesser behavior. Susan Garrett calls these "screw up cookies."

  Put the dog away and try again another day. Often you will see the dog suddenly get it in the next session. Some trainers, including myself, refer to this phenomenon as "latent learning." We see this in humans, too. You go to bed with a problem on your mind and wake up with understanding. It also works with our dogs.

- *Important:* Do not lure the dog onto the book with food. It is better to reinforce approximations of the behavior in the center over the book. Placing the reinforcement in the center of the perch begins to direct the dog's attention to the center of the perch—the place we want him to step up onto. But please don't lure.

- Always feed low and in the middle of the book. This is ultimately where we want the dog to be. Operant conditioning expert Bob Bailey says, "Click for action, but reward for position" and that is exactly what you are doing.

- *Do not put a command on the behavior.* Keep in mind: The word will not create the behavior. Dogs learn by being reinforced, not by being told what to do. The cues for the behavior are simply the presentation of the phonebook and the proximity of the handler's body to the book.

Especially early in training with perches, it helps the dog orient toward the perch if you reinforce any interaction with it low and in the center of the perch.

- Teach this behavior in short segments of a couple of minutes followed by a break. Put the dog in a crate for a half hour or so and then work him again. You will find that the short sessions followed by the crate time enhances the dog's ability to learn the task. The crate is not punishment. Studies have shown that learning is enhanced when you allow your dog to relax and avoid stimulation by other things.

Here are some steps your dog might offer in getting onto the perch. You may find that your dog tries some or all of these behaviors or gets on the perch the first time he sees it. Whatever happens, be ready to reinforce his efforts.

- Looks at the phonebook
- Sniffs it
- Touches it
- Steps over it
- Touches it with a foot
- Puts a foot on the book
- Puts two feet on the book

In the shaping process, remember that your dog is *on the way* to learning a behavior. You need to strike a balance between giving him enough information (clicks and reinforcement) to guide him along the way and rewarding one step in the process enough that the dog interprets that step as the end goal. If your dog

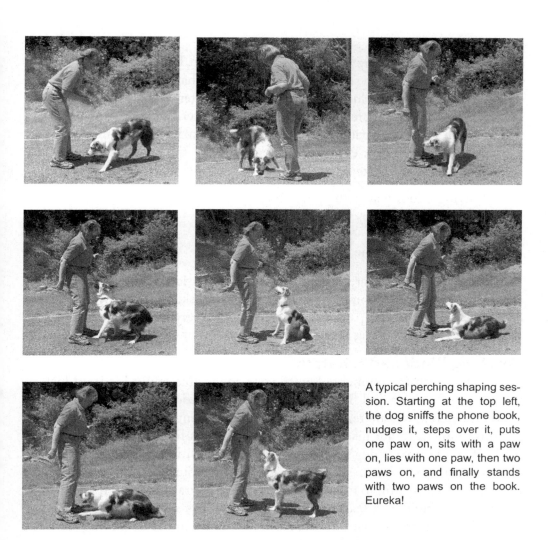

A typical perching shaping session. Starting at the top left, the dog sniffs the phone book, nudges it, steps over it, puts one paw on, sits with a paw on, lies with one paw, then two paws on, and finally stands with two paws on the book. Eureka!

thinks one step is the end goal, he'll get stuck. Especially when you start, it helps to reinforce totally new behaviors (like pushing the phonebook along the floor with his nose), even if they aren't terribly relevant. It helps communicate that experimenting with the phonebook is rewarded and builds a positive association with it. When you get a good response, try to get a couple of repetitions, but then quickly up the ante: ask for a little bit more—or something different. Shaping can proceed quickly, and it's generally a good sign if it does.

Remain open-minded and practice each step until you are satisfied that the dog is getting the idea. Be ready for leaps in understanding. Be particularly attentive *every moment* you are working with the dog and watch for signs of understanding so you can reward, and then up the ante and go to the next step. However if your dog starts making errors, for instance, offering two to three incorrect responses for a step, stop immediately and return to an easier step. Do not frustrate your dog with this game. Break each step down into a smaller behavior. Most clicker trainers advise, "Be a splitter, not a lumper." This means it is better to break down behaviors into smaller sections that are easier for the dog to master and lead to quick success than to lump several behaviors into one big step that may totally confuse the dog and try your patience. For example, putting a foot on the book could be broken down into the following steps:

- Moving a foot nearer the phonebook

- Lifting a foot

- Reaching toward the book with a foot

Be conscious and aware during each training session. Don't talk to anyone, answer the phone, or become distracted from your task. Shaping is concentrated detail work. You must be paying close attention to everything your dog is doing. Remember to keep training sessions short and give your dog frequent breaks.

Teaching Hindquarter Rotation

Practice with the phonebook until your dog is able to put his front feet on it from any direction and from 2' to 3' away. Once you have taught the dog to get on the perch, you are ready to use the universal language of pressure to start teaching him to rotate his hindquarters around his front feet on the phonebook. If you face your dog's right side and step slightly toward him with your left leg, remember that *the pressure* from moving your body toward the dog's rear legs will cause him to move his hindquarters laterally to the left, *away* from that pressure. He'll have learned to keep his front legs on the phone book—and now he'll also learn to pivot on the phone book. So in the beginning as you're watching for movement of the hindquarters, face your dog's side. It also allows you to see the steps along the way.

The steps may look something like this:

1. Dog shuffles a hind foot in either direction

2. Dog takes one step right or left

3. Dog takes two steps right or left

4. Takes three steps right or left

5. Dog begins to move right and/or left in response to the handler's position

  - Dog moves to the left if handler is on his right

  - Dog moves to the right if handler is on his left

6. Dog reliably moves his body in response to the pressure he feels when the handler moves toward him

Keep your focus on your dog's back legs. Look for any movement in any direction. Start by reinforcing simple, small movements of the hindquarters. You must pay careful attention since movements happen quickly at first. Be ready to mark and reinforce any and all movements in the direction of your final behavior. Remember to teach this skill on both sides so that your dog moves away from the pressure of your body from either direction.

Understanding Shoulder Cues

Rotation of the handler's shoulders also plays a vital role in directing the dog's path and position in teaching the turn on the forehand. Competition obedience has taught me that movement—especially the rotation—of the shoulders plays a critical role in cueing turns and the dog's position in relation to his handler. At first I didn't understand why so many dogs at heel lagged behind their handlers. Then I realized that, when a dog fell slightly behind the handler, the handler tended to look back at the dog. Turning the head to the left to look back at the dog unintentionally rotated the left shoulder to the rear, applying pressure to the dog. The dog picked up this unconscious cue to stay behind the handler, so continued to lag.

This knowledge of dog communication applies as well to the world of agility. Rotating your shoulders applies—or releases—pressure on the dog. If you rotate your shoulder back toward the dog behind you or at your side, it acts to block him, keeping him behind you, because the dog reads the rotation as pressure toward him. If you rotate your shoulder away from the dog, he will tend to come toward you, since you are "inviting" him into your space. You can execute same-side turns more easily by rotating your shoulders in the direction of the turn and away from the dog, which cues the dog to turn toward—and with—you.

Keep these shoulder dynamics in mind when teaching your dog to rotate his hindquarters toward you and away from you. Although at first you'll use your whole body to cue the dog to move his hindquarters toward or away from you, soon you will be able use the shoulder nearest his hindquarters to signal the direction you want him to turn simply by rotating it forward or backward.

With practice, your dog will learn to turn on the forehand in a little arc at your side, keying off your shoulder movements.

Initially, in the case above where you're facing the dog's right side, it helps to indicate with the hand nearest the hindquarters (left) which direction you want him to rotate. Use the leg nearest the hindquarters (left) to step toward the dog and rotate the left shoulder forward as well.

If the handler applies pressure by stepping and rotating her shoulders toward the dog's rear, the dog moves his hindquarters away from the pressure. Watch the shifts in the handler's shoulders and feet and in the dog's hind legs.

Once your dog is extremely proficient at moving away from you with his front end on the perch, it's time to teach him to rotate *toward* your body instead of *away* from it. Again, start facing the dog's side. I help my dog by indicating with the hand closest to the dog's hindquarters the direction I want him to rotate. With the leg nearest the dog's rear, I then step a *few inches away from him*, rotate the shoulder closest to his hindquarters back slightly, and wait. If I were facing my dog's right side, I would bring my left hand toward my body,

If the handler removes pressure by stepping and rotating her shoulders away from the dog's rear, the dog swings his hindquarters toward the handler. Watch the shifts in the handler's shoulders and feet and in the dog's hind legs.

step back on my left foot and rotate my left shoulder back. Rotating the shoulder back removes pressure, inviting the dog into your space and becomes the ultimate cue for the dog, in this case, for pivoting his hindquarters to the right, toward you. Watch for any motion of the hind leg that closes the gap between you and the dog and reinforce that initial behavior. Since the dog is already quite proficient at rotating in either direction, he will learn the cue quickly.

When your dog can rotate toward and away from you on both the right and left side while standing with his forefeet on the phonebook, you can start to fade the perch. Begin to fade or minimize your perch/book until your dog will target and rotate on a simple piece of paper. With continued practice you can make the paper smaller and smaller until your dog is easily rotating his hindquarters primarily from your shoulder rotation cues. By gradually shifting your angle to the dog so that you end up in heel position rather than facing his side, you then can train your dog to turn on the forehand toward and away from you solely off your shoulder cues. Take your time with this transition—remember your dog's perspective on the cue will change as you change your position from facing his side to standing side-by-side with him in heel position. The finished picture will be a dog that rotates with you at your side—forward or backward—following your near shoulder movement. That means that if your dog is on your left and you rotate your near (left) shoulder back, he will rotate his hind legs back and to the right while his forelegs pivot in place, following the arc of your body. He is following the pressure of the rotation toward him while maintaining heel position. Congratulate yourself when you reach this goal! It will come in handy in the next chapter.

Chapter 4: Circle Work for Agility

Training obedience dogs for many years has taught me to be sensitive to the difficulty dogs have with circle patterns and the changes of pace they require. For instance, heeling in a tight clockwise circle (with the dog on my left on the outside of the circle) requires him to increase his pace and bend his body to the right in order to stay with me. Likewise, heeling in a counterclockwise circle (the dog on my left on the inside) necessitates that he travel at a slower pace, bending his body to conform to the curve. Watch dogs in the obedience ring as they perform left and right turns, about turns, and the Figure Eight exercise. It is evident that many a handler has not taught her dog what to do with his body to successfully execute these difficult maneuvers. Dogs often crab (angle their rear end away from the handler and out of alignment), bump the handler, forge, or lag—all because they have received insufficient training and reinforcement for the exact performance of staying in position while turning in a circle with the handler.

In the equestrian world, however, work in large and small circles constitutes a major part of many competitions such as reining or dressage. A rider spends hundreds of hours in the saddle perfecting circles so his horse is fluid and is able to bend his body around the circle. Circle and bending work is crucial for the young horse and should also be for our agility dogs. After all, agility often presents even more challenging patterns than obedience—at a much faster pace.

Photo Credit: Bill Weismann

It's important for horses to be supple so they can turn tightly. Here a rider turns her horse, working on bending his body to the right.

Agility, however, differs from obedience in that the dog works on both sides of the handler so he must learn to execute circles from *four* different perspectives:

1. Clockwise circles on our left (dog on the outside)

2. Clockwise circles on our right (dog on the inside)

3. Counterclockwise circles on our left (dog on the inside)

4. Counterclockwise circles on our right (dog on the outside)

Teaching your dog independent movement of the hindquarters pays off when you start heeling in tight circles. The dog will be able bend his body as well as keep pace with you.

Before beginning your circle work you may find it helpful to know how supple your dog's spine is. Here is an exercise to help your dog learn to bend his spine. With one hand hold the dog tightly against the front of your legs. With the other hand lure his head toward his tail so that you are bending the dog (and his spine) around your hand. Do this several times on one side and then turn the dog around and bend in the other direction. You will probably notice that your dog is suppler (more easily bent) on one side than the other. Be sure to stretch him more on the stiff side so your dog can bend easily on either side.

How supple is your dog's spine? By holding your dog snugly against your legs and luring his head toward his rear, you can determine if he bends more easily in one direction than the other. If he does bend more easily in one direction, plan on exercising the stiffer side more.

Large Circles: Dog on the Outside

Lay out a circle about 60' in diameter. You can use soccer cones, bricks, poles, or anything that helps you see a round path. Begin with the dog on your left traveling in a clockwise direction (he'll be heading around the outside of the circle so will have to travel slightly *faster* than you). This is going to be the easiest circle and will set the stage for everything else. Start walking the course you have laid out at a normal pace with your body in correct position, upright and just *slightly ahead* of the vertical. Your left arm should be in the soft L-position we discussed earlier. Hide food from sight in your closed left hand and use the pointing finger of this lead hand to draw the path for your dog.

Reinforce your dog generously every couple of steps as he remains with you, keeping his body in the correct position. At this point, if he is able to bend his body slightly in an arc, be sure to reinforce that behavior. Once he begins to figure out that he is turning in a circle, he may be more inclined to round his body around the arc. Be sure to reinforce at your pants seam and watch for any tendency to crab, forge, or lag. Be careful that you do not reinforce these behaviors at any time.

As you are walking, be sure to think about the following:

1. Remember your goal: the behavior you are reinforcing is your dog *picking up* his pace so he can stay with you and maintain his position beside your body. The most important criterion is the increased pace because he is walking a path that is larger than yours.

2. Note your body while you are walking. Are you in the correct position?

    *   Pay attention to the position of your head, shoulders, and body. Your head should be very slightly inclined toward the dog so you can see him and where you are going. Your shoulders, body, and feet should be traveling along the line of the circle. Remember your body is setting the path for the dog. You are both looking forward and at your dog. It may take some practice but it is an important skill.

    *   Your stride for this exercise should be rhythmic, about two steps per second, which will give you a nice brisk pace to work with.

Pay attention to *where* you are reinforcing the dog. Your reinforcement should come from the hand next to the dog and should be within a 4" range from your body, at the place where you want the dog to remain. At this stage I still tend to stop and reinforce at my pants' seam to encourage the dog to remain close by my side.

When heeling in circles with your dog, make sure you focus where you want to go and that your head, shoulders, and feet communicate that direction to your dog.

After you have gone around the circle several times, turn toward the dog and pick him up with your right hand, in the same position as your left hand was, so he is tracking on the outside of the circle heading in the opposite direction. Walk the circle at your normal pace reinforcing generously every four to five steps along the way.

Continue to practice until you have reinforced sufficiently and the dog is comfortable in his position beside you. You should see him slightly increase his pace so he can stay beside you since he is traveling a larger circle than you and must adjust his pace accordingly. This is just the beginning of teaching pace changes relative to your body, your path, and your pace. More is on the way.

Large Circles: Dog on Inside

When the dog is on the inside of the circle, your path is now larger than his and again he must adjust his pace accordingly. Now he must *slow down* in order to stay with you. Begin walking the large circle counterclockwise at your normal pace with your dog on your left side, reinforcing generously every four to five steps at first. Keep your dog on your left and reinforce about 10 times. Then turn toward your dog and pick him up on your right hand. Begin traveling the circle clockwise at a normal pace with your dog on the inside, reinforcing generously every four to five steps.

Continue working at a walk. Be crystal clear to your dog when you communicate with your body cues. Keep your body upright but because your dog needs to slow down, your body position should be slightly *behind the vertical*. Remember, you are also giving your dog information about his correct behavior through your food reinforcement, so it is essential that you know what you are reinforcing. Watch for and generously reward his adjusting and slowing down his pace in response to your body cues.

When you and the dog are able to successfully perform large circles both clockwise and counterclockwise with the dog on either side of you, you are ready to introduce pace changes.

Large Circles: Changes of Pace

Once you are ready to begin pace changes in large circles, please go back and reread the "Fast Pace" and "Slow Pace" sections for straight-line heeling. Apply those guidelines to your large circle work, but please don't take shortcuts. You'll only have to start over again later.

Teaching pace changes on large circles by altering your body position (tilting ahead of and behind the vertical) will help you greatly when you begin to run courses. You will have a valuable tool that will enable you to adjust your dog's pace on course if, for example, he is traveling a lateral distance away from you and must collect himself for a difficult weave pole entry. This heeling skill also supports and gives information to the dog early when a tricky turn or maneuver is coming up on course. It is particularly important for fast, high-drive dogs that need to know about course and speed changes as early as possible to adjust their speed. The ability to cue a dog in extended stride (when he is running fast and jumping flat and long) to collect his stride (to run slower and jump shorter and rounder) is an extremely valuable skill. Teaching beginning skills on the flat can save many an off-course later on. I can tell you from personal experience that this skill has saved me many times with Pippin, my high-drive Border Collie.

Small Circles

Small circle work will teach you how to give early body cues for upcoming tricky sequences and teach your dog how to negotiate tight sequences. For such sequences, you must cue your dog at least one or two obstacles ahead of time. And the faster the dog, the earlier you must give the cue. If the dog learns to read the cues early, he can set up before the obstacle and avoid costly mistakes or injuries.

Teaching flatwork in small circles is similar to teaching flatwork in large ones—*your body is your cue to the dog*. The main difference is that the dog not only has to adjust his pace but also more noticeably has to bend his body to keep aligned with yours. This is where training of independent movement of the hindquarters really pays off. When executing small circles, your head, shoulders, legs, and feet cue the dog about where he is to go and what he is to do. In competition heeling, it is important to look in the direction you want the dog to go. In agility, your focus is even more critical since this cue can give early information to the dog.

Set up a small circle about 10' in diameter. If you are working outside, use some cornstarch to create a circle on grass. Practice walking circles without your dog—in both directions. Think about the position of your head, shoulders, hands, and body and about how you will use your body to cue your dog. The hand farthest from the dog will be relaxed and at your side while the hand nearest the dog will be in a relaxed L-shape next to your side. Your shoulders will be square along the arc of the circle. And your head will be watching where you are going *and* where your dog is. When you are sure you can do your job, it's time to get your dog.

Small Circles: Dog on the Outside and Inside

With your dog on your left start walking a small circle clockwise at a normal pace. Show the path to your dog using the pointing finger of your lead hand. The goal is for your dog to speed up and slightly bend his body around you to keep up with you. Mark and reinforce this behavior after a few steps. Repeat several times on the left. Turn toward the dog, pick him up on the right, and repeat on the right going counterclockwise. Continue practicing until your dog is able to *stay in position* for four to five complete rotations on either side.

Caution: It is tempting for the beginning handler teaching this behavior to her dog to *look back* toward the dog if he is not completely aligned by her leg. Be aware of this bad habit so you don't develop it. Looking back at your dog pushes your shoulder back and actually signals your dog to stay behind you. He interprets the shoulder movement as pressure toward him. Remember our discussion about shoulder cues in Chapter 3? Your shoulders provide critical information for the dog so keep them square and facing straight ahead, not rotating backward toward the dog. If your dog *is* having lagging problems, take a step and then reinforce *slightly ahead of your seam*. Reinforce in this way for a day or so until your dog understands where he is to be. Once your dog understands, you will be able to return to reinforcing at your seam.

Working in small circles requires your dog both to bend more and to keep pace with you. It's challenging for your dog to learn to do both well. If your dog lags, you may be tempted to look back at him, as Levenson is demonstrating here. But glancing back at a lagging dog rotates your near shoulder back toward the dog, applying pressure that makes the dog lag even further behind. Keep your head facing forward in the direction you want to go.

Now put your dog on the inside of the small circle and practice in both directions as you did on the outside of the circle. Remember your body cues. Your dog has to bend his body even more to stay aligned with you. Here your dog's work on the phonebook will enable him to easily rotate his hindquarters to stay parallel and even with you. Start out very slowly, perhaps one step at a time. Be sure to reinforce generously when your dog begins to offer a turn on the forehand. Your criteria should be clear in your mind. Your dog should maintain position without forging or lagging and keep his hindquarters along an arc beside you.

Small Circles with Pace Changes

Pace changes become more challenging as the diameter of the circle shrinks and as you combine straight-line heeling with circle work. In this exercise, you lead your dog into a small circle on a straight line and exit on a straight line. In particular, as you increase your pace, watch for crabbing and bumping. It's a hard task for your dog to both adjust his pace and bend his body in line with the circle to keep aligned with you. Teaching your dog to slow down when coming into the circle and to speed up when exiting it is readily applicable to executing complex maneuvers on course.

Start with the dog on your left. Heel the dog in a straight line at a normal pace for several steps. Turn left and walk a small 10' circle to the left. Cue your dog by turning your head and body *just before* you make the turn. In other words, look where you will be going a second before you begin the turn. The dog will have to slow down and rotate his hindquarters to stay with you. Mark and reward the instant you see him slow down and meet your criteria.

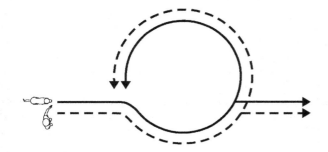

Since small circle work trains the dog to respond to your cues and work fluidly in tight spaces, once he's mastered the circles, the next step is to challenge him to get in and out of them with ease. Use brisk straight-line heeling to enter and exit small circles, making sure your dog adjusts his pace in the circle accordingly.

Continue walking the rest of the circle and exit to straight-line heeling at a normal pace. Your dog should speed up as you leave the circle. Stop, mark, and reinforce your dog for that behavior. You can help your dog learn to control his pace more quickly if you use your upper body to cue acceleration and deceleration. Be sure to mark the correct response the moment you see it. Stop frequently and reinforce the dog generously in the early stages to accelerate his learning.

Practice until your dog can automatically slow down and speed up in the circle according to your body cues. Practice this exercise with your dog on both the left and right and on the inside and outside of the circle. A dog that learns to respond precisely to your cues to adjust his pace and position makes a facile and flexible teammate.

Chapter 5: Advanced Flatwork for Agility

Obedience handlers use many exercises to teach dogs to follow the handler's body. These exercises have direct applications for agility dogs. One such exercise—called the figure eight exercise—teaches the dog to extend and then to collect his stride. Another important extension/collection exercise is called the serpentine. I believe both of these exercises help an agility dog become more responsive to his handler.

The Figure Eight Exercise

The figure eight exercise is a heeling exercise around two people ("posts") standing in the ring about 8' apart. The dog and handler travel a figure eight path around the posts and are judged on the dog's ability to adjust his pace and keep aligned with his handler since the figure eight path forces him to shift between the inside and outside of small circles while receiving only subtle cues from the handler's body. Used in agility training, this skill helps dogs to maneuver in tight spaces.

Set up two cones or two jump standards, 8' to 10' apart. With your dog on your left, start at a normal pace and show the dog the path with your pointed finger. Walk the path shown in the figure below.

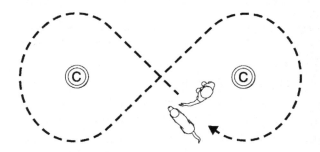

The figure eight and serpentine exercises require rapid shifts between working on the inside and outside of small circles and thus offer excellent practice in making those transitions smoothly and accurately. A dog that can master these exercises can handle tight wraps, sharp shoulder pulls, threadles, and other such course challenges with greater ease.

Reinforce your dog every three to four steps as he adjusts his pace and his hindquarters to stay with you. Reward frequently and generously at varying intervals along the path. You want to pay particular attention to the outside and inside turns. Reinforce for slowing down and rotating the hindquarters on the inside turn and for speeding up and staying aligned on the outside one.

Here Levenson uses correct body language and her near-index finger to help her dog keep closely aligned on the outside curve of the figure eight, where dogs tend to swing wide and fall behind.

To keep from bumping Levenson on the inside curve of the figure eight, her dog must slow his pace and bend his body. Again, her body language and hand signals are critical in keeping him aligned.

Next turn toward the dog, pick him up on your right and repeat. Your work with the small circles should make this transition easier for both you and your dog. With the figure eight exercise it is not necessary to work with any pace beyond a normal pace because in agility we rarely if ever run in spaces tighter than 8'. By varying the size and increasing the difficulty of the figure eight exercise, however, you can help teach your dog about collection and extension. If you increase the size of the figure eight to 16' or 24', you can accelerate and decelerate at strategic places and your dog will learn to extend or collect his stride accordingly.

Serpentines for Agility

I love serpentines. They are valuable teaching tools for dogs. Serpentines teach a dog to slow down, speed up, and change pace depending on how you turn, walk, and run. A typical serpentine uses several cones 8' to 10' apart in the following pattern:

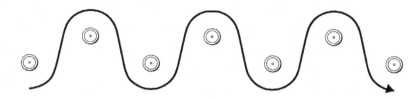

With the dog on his left, the handler follows the pattern indicated, teaching the dog to vary his pace through the obstacles. The dog must speed up on the outside and slow down and rotate his hindquarters on the inside.

Try this exercise first at a walk with the dog on your left and then with the dog on your right. Remember to reinforce at key points where the dog has offered to speed up, slow down, and bend his body through the course. Again, if you vary the size of the serpentine you can add acceleration through the straightaways and outside turns and deceleration on the inside turns. Get creative and watch your dog become quite adept at following your body and cues.

Chapter 6: Front and Rear Crosses: Changes of Side, Changes of Lead

Changes of side or front and rear crosses are needed to complete your understanding of flatwork. To understand why learning how to perform front and rear crosses is important, you need to know what actually is happening when a handler executes a crossing turn. Most people know that there is a change of side. The handler may change from the right side of the dog to the left and vice versa. But many beginners don't detect that there also is something crucial happening with the dog: a change of lead.

Handlers who come from an equestrian background clearly understand leads and changes of lead. You'll see a lead when a horse is cantering in circles. The horse

The front lead leg is the one that hits the ground last. For the horse cantering on the flat, the right front is the lead leg. The horse landing off the jump is on his left lead.

The dog (left) is cantering on his left lead. The lead leg helps the dog pivot, much as leaning into a turn helps a motorcycle rider make the turn. The dog (right) has landed correctly off the jump on her right lead so that she can make the tight turn to the next jump to the right.

travels into the circle leading with a particular foreleg (the last one to touch the ground). A right lead means that the horse is going in a clockwise direction leading with the right foreleg. A left lead is just the reverse. When the horse switches from moving clockwise to counterclockwise, he changes leads. It's a matter of balance: the horse would feel off-balance if he tried to canter clockwise on a left lead. It is sometimes more difficult to see leads in dogs because their legs are so much smaller and move faster, but recognizing which lead a dog is on (or should be expected to be on) can help a handler set up the dog for a sequence. A lot of spinning after jumps and even refusals at jumps or tunnels result when the dog is on the wrong lead because the handler failed to cue the dog in time about an upcoming change of direction. A dog will be properly balanced when cantering on the correct lead and will flow more naturally on a course. Practicing crosses will train your dog to respond to your cues for a lead change.

As with a horse, when your dog is traveling a clockwise circle he is on the right lead. When traveling in a counterclockwise circle, he's on the left lead. So when you perform a front cross or a rear cross with your dog, you are also changing his lead. You will see the importance of this concept when we start putting small sequences together and considering whether sequences arc to the left or to the right.

There are as many ways to teach crossing turns as there are teachers who teach them. In my classes I break the crosses down into small parts and introduce each step bit by bit. I also start by teaching front and rear crosses on the flat. A beginning handler can execute either a front or a rear cross on the flat, allowing him the flexibility to handle today's Novice and even Open classes efficiently. The handler can further expand this foundation as his and his dog's abilities grow.

Front Crosses

A front cross is usually performed with the handler ahead of the dog although, as you will soon see, you can also perform a front cross when running beside the dog. I teach front crosses without any jumps or distractions so the handler can think about what she is doing both with her dog and with her own body.

Here are directions for initiating a front cross with your dog from your left to your right side. I always use the same side hand and leg for cueing my dog. This tends to make your body language coherent. Teach yourself the front cross step by step so that it becomes natural to you and you don't have to think about it.

1. Begin with your imaginary dog on your left and with food in both hands. Step forward on the left leg with your leading left hand drawing the path for your dog.

2. Cue the turn. Reach across your body with your right hand as though pointing to the dog's nose and with your stiff index finger, give a pick-up cue. This hand signal eventually will become your cue indicating an upcoming change of side, but for now you simply want to stop your dog's forward momentum, catch his attention, and make him turn toward you. At the same time, step forward at a 45° angle toward your dog with your right foot (the foot that will become the "near" foot) and drop your left hand and shoulder.

3. Step back and behind onto your left foot, weight on your left leg, as your imaginary dog completes his turn toward you and pick him up on your right hand.

4. Step forward on your right foot and extend your right hand (no higher than your waist) as though pointing toward the next obstacle, completing the cross. Your imaginary dog now should be on your right side, parallel with your body.

Front cross with dog on left, without obstacles: Levenson reaches across her body and cues a pick-up with her right hand as she turns toward her dog and steps forward at an angle with her right foot. In response, the dog turns toward her as she steps back on her left foot and continues turning left. As the dog tucks into her right side, she steps forward with her right foot.

Please practice the footwork and hand signals many times without your dog. This exercise helps you better concentrate on and train your dog. If you try training both yourself *and* your dog at the same time, most likely you will confuse and stress your dog. If you are clear about your job, you can begin to think about giving information and reinforcing your dog at appropriate places. When you feel you are ready to introduce your dog to the picture, be sure to have food in both hands so you can reward several times during each step of the learning process. Because of the many new steps in the front cross, a high rate of reinforcement helps your dog pay attention to the information you are teaching him.

Here are some places to reward your dog:

- Step One: Reinforce as you step forward on your left foot.

- Step Two: Reward with your right hand as you cue the turn and your dog turns toward you. Remember you are also dropping your left hand and shoulder (an important cue) and stepping back on your left foot.

- Step Three: Reinforce your dog as you pick him up on your right side.

- Step Four: As you step forward on your right foot and extend your right hand (as though indicating the next obstacle), reward your dog again for changing leads and lining up on your right side.

Front cross with dog and obstacles: The pace is faster and the distances between handler and dog are greater so the body cues need to be more pronounced, but the principles are the same.

Several years ago Kathy Keats gave me a valuable hint. She said that people often fail to reinforce the dog for responding to their handling cues. It helps your dog learn to respond to the front cross if you reward him for reacting to your changing body position and hand signals in this exercise. Once again you are isolating and emphasizing a piece of handling and telling the dog, "Pay attention here. It's important." As a result, your dog will begin to look for (and respond to) these important handling cues.

Performing the front cross from the right side to the left side is simply the process in reverse.

1. Begin with your dog on your right. Step forward on your right leg with your right hand drawing the path for your dog.

2. Cue the turn. Reach across your body with your left hand giving the pick-up signal, which will be your cue indicating the change of side, and step forward at a 45° angle toward your dog with your left foot (the foot you will be changing to that will become the near foot). At the same time drop your right hand and right shoulder.

3. Step back onto your right foot, weight on your right leg, and, as your dog turns toward you, pick him up on your left hand.

4. Step forward on your left foot and extend your left hand (as though toward the next obstacle) completing the cross.

Keep your reinforcement rate high and reward at the same strategic places you used in teaching the front cross that began on your left.

Rear Crosses

Rear crosses are just as critical in performing agility courses as are front crosses, particularly if you are running a fast dog. Giving your dog "permission" to go ahead of you and take a particular piece of equipment allows you to cross behind him and move to another part of the course so that you can better direct your dog. There are many who believe that front crosses are faster than rear crosses. I remember an fascinating test of this in the highly competitive 24" class of the 2006 AKC National Agility finals. Marcus Topps and Juice ran the course in 30.928 seconds using rear crosses. Gerry Brown and Sterling ran the same course in 30.817 seconds using front crosses. Although Gerry won the class, the time difference between the two men was a statistically insignificant .111 of a second.

Slower dogs should also be taught the correct execution of a rear cross even if they are less likely to be moving ahead of you. Current designs of advanced courses are intended to challenge your handling. Being able to perform a rear cross is often the best choice on a course. I think handlers should have both front and rear crosses in their repertoire and the dog should be comfortable with both.

The following pictures illustrate how I teach a rear cross to my dogs. Unlike with the front cross, I build the rear cross in successive stages. The first is *teaching the dog to bend in a circle*. The second is *cueing the dog to bend in a circle and turn away from you* as you step in behind him. The third is *cueing the turn*. As with front crosses I always start with food in both hands.

1. *Teach the dog to bend in a circle:* To execute a successful rear cross, your dog's spine must be flexible, so train him to arc away from you in a full circle at your side. Don't worry about your footwork for now.

- With your dog on your left and using only your left hand, draw a path that brings the dog slightly in front of your body and around in a counterclockwise circle (360°).

Rear cross with dog on left, without obstacles: The first three frames show Levenson using her left hand to turn the dog counterclockwise; the last three frames show her picking up the dog on her right hand as she steps in behind to complete the cross.

- Reinforce.
- Continue until the dog will easily complete a circle slightly in front of your body. To perform a rear cross, your dog needs to be ahead of you so you can cross behind him.

2. *Turn the dog in a 180° arc away from you:* Your dog doesn't turn in a full circle for a rear cross. A 180° turn (semicircle) is what you need. Don't worry about your footwork.

- With your dog on your left and using only your left hand, draw a counterclockwise path that brings the dog slightly in front of your body and around in a 180° arc away from you.
- Your dog will then be facing in the opposite direction from you. Reinforce his head position.
- If your dog has difficulty in bending, practice the spine flexibility exercise on page 52.

The cue for a rear cross becomes the dropped near shoulder as the hand describes the turn away from the handler by flipping the hand palm up. Once the dog is committed to the jump, the turn, and the lead change, the handler steps in behind and uses her off arm to pick up her dog on the opposite side.

Rear cross with dog and obstacles: For effective rear crosses, the dog must be comfortable being sent ahead and must learn the shoulder and hand signal. A green dog that doesn't recognize the rear-cross cue often turns in the new direction only as his handler actually crosses behind him, which may cause the dog to drop a bar or to bobble the switch of sides and lead.

3. *Turn the dog away as you turn with him:*
   - With the dog on your left side, step forward on your left foot, signaling with your left hand for your dog to turn away in a 180° arc from you.
   - As your dog bends to the left, cross over and step in behind his tail, pick him up on your right hand, and reinforce.

4. *Turn the dog away with a body cue:*
   - With the dog on your left side, step forward on your left foot, drop (lower) your left shoulder, and signal with your left hand for your dog to turn away in a 180° arc from you. (The shoulder drop and directional cue of your hand "flipping" the dog away from you eventually will become the rear-cross cue for the dog.)
   - Just as you did above in step three, as the dog turns left immediately cross over with your opposite foot, crossing behind the dog's tail.
   - As you step in behind your dog, pick him up on the right hand and reinforce.

5. *Fade the cue:*
   - Eventually you can fade the cue so that you are left with a shoulder drop and a "flip" in the direction you want the dog to go. It helps to think of leaning into the turn with your shoulder; your hand will follow.

Begin with reinforcement for each step. Once the dog begins to understand the turn, you can initiate the turn with your left shoulder and follow through with the hand flip as the dog turns. When comfortable on one side, repeat the mirror image on the opposite side. Notice where your dog is the weakest, and practice more often on your dog's weaker side.

Chapter 7: Looking Ahead

Once you have your flatwork foundation in place it is time to begin adding some simple but crucial sequences that will further develop your teamwork. The training sequences on these pages are just suggestions for using flatwork in your course work. Many "Backyard Dog" articles in *Clean Run* magazine are perfect for the transition from flatwork to sequence and course work.

Here are some guidelines to help with the transition:

- Keep your near hand in the relaxed L-position we described earlier to draw the path for your dog.

- Your hand next to the dog is considered your lead hand and should do just that—lead the dog. Imagine that you have a laser pointer attached to your finger that is painting the path for the dog. That means your hand should always be slightly ahead of the dog so he can tell where he is to go. I often remind handlers that they don't need to point at the dog. He already knows where he is. He just doesn't know where he is going. That's your job with your handling.

- Your hand and arm are really just an extension of your shoulders that should be square to the path you want the dog to take.

- Make sure your feet are facing in the direction you want your dog to go. Develop the habit now of thinking about your feet. For now, your entire body should be consistent in its message.

Integrating obstacles into flatwork makes timely communication imperative if the dog is to stay on course and clear jumps. Right off the start here, the dog is prepared for the 90° turn to the right for the second jump. She's jumping the first jump at an angle, and Levenson continues that line until she squares up for the second jump. As the dog launches toward the second jump, Levenson has turned her body slightly to the right, cueing the dog to the next 90° turn to the final jump.

Just as we did with the flatwork, starting with straight-line sequences works best.

Straight-line Work

Figure A shows a good exercise to begin your shift into sequences. If you have started your dog in jumping you can begin with the jumps at a low height—4" for small dogs and 8" to 12" for larger dogs. If you have not started jumping because you have a puppy or for any other reason, you can still perform these exercises with the dog just running between the stanchions. Height or jumping is not the issue; handling is. You want to teach your dog to follow you now with the distraction of jumps.

Start 4' to 6' away from the first jump with your dog either on your left or right. As you make the transition out of flatwork, start with your dog standing beside you. Walk with your dog toward the first jump leading your dog with your hand and your body. At a walk your body should be just slightly inclined forward. Walk straight ahead and, with your near hand drawing the path, send your dog over the jumps (or through the stanchions). At the end of the sequence reward your dog with the hand closest to him. Be sure to reinforce down your pants' seam, facing the direction you were headed. Now turn toward your dog, pick him up on the other side, and repeat the sequence heading back in the other direction. Stay at a walk for several repetitions. Your dog should be moving beside you and staying between the stanchions. When he is successful you can start to increase speed gradually, first to a slow jog, being certain to incline your body forward a bit more. Every time you increase your speed be sure also to increase the forward incline of your body.

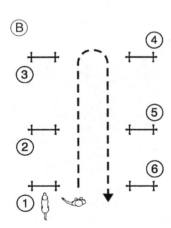

Straight Lines to Turns

Once you are executing straight lines successfully you are ready to add a turn. In **Figure B** I simply added a 180° turn at the end of two straight lines of jumps. Here is where it can get a little tricky so you must first practice without your dog. To execute the turn efficiently, the dog needs to know *before the #3 jump* that the turn is coming up. One of the best ways to cue the upcoming turn is by a change in your body position and footwork. As your dog comes over the second jump, you will need to straighten your body and adjust your footwork thus indicating a change to a slower pace. Practice without your dog. Immediately after you visualize the dog landing off the second jump, straighten up and switch to a walk. Walk through the turn, then incline your body forward and pick up your pace for the second piece of straight-line work. Make sure your head, shoulders, and feet all communicate the change in direction.

Timely communication helps the dog turn cleanly. Here, Levenson demonstrates what happens when she only begins to turn toward the next jump after her dog has landed going straight off the first jump. Her dog turns so wide it is unlikely she can make the next jump.

In a second try, Levenson is already turning toward the second jump as her dog clears the first one. In response, the dog starts to turn in the air, lands turning on her right lead, and follows a tighter line to the second jump. She'll still have to scramble but she can make the next jump.

Learning to change body and foot position in a clear and timely manner is a critical part of course work and should be practiced until you don't have to think about it. Often we see dogs run well past the point where they should have turned because the handler did not cue the dog about the upcoming turn. Once you are able to carry out your part effectively, you are ready to add your dog.

In order to develop a good understanding of this skill, break the exercise down into smaller steps. Remember Bob Bailey's advice: "Be a splitter, not a lumper." Reward each little step to help your dog understand faster what you want. For example, reinforce after the second jump when the dog recognizes and slows down as you straighten up your body and adjust your footwork.

Don't worry about finishing the sequence. Remember Kathy Keats's suggestion that we reinforce understanding of our cues? This is the perfect place to practice her advice. After reinforcing several times for your dog's slowing down, add the turn and reward at various steps during the turn. Once you have your dog paying attention and expecting reinforcement, add the change to a fast pace in the straightaway. Be sure to reward there also. In other words, don't just reinforce the whole sequence. Find places within the sequence where your dog has shown understanding and responded and reward him there also.

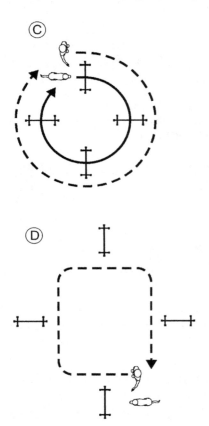

Circle Work

The four-jump setup in **Figure C** is terrific for practicing circle work with your dog. The dog should travel a circle through the sequence but in the beginning it is best if the handler's path is a square as in the larger circle of jumps shown in **Figure D**. Handling the sequence in this way, with the dog on the outside, helps a handler keep his shoulders and body square until the dog is committed to the turn and thus helps cue the dog more effectively. When the dog commits to the turn, the jump should be straight ahead and both dog and handler will be headed in that direction. Practicing this skill also prevents you from rotating your body too early and pulling the dog off the jump.

To start, set the jumps about 10' to 12' apart. In this exercise the dog is running on the outside. Sit the dog about 3' from the jump on either your right or your left, depending on your direction. Step a few feet to the dog's side so you will not run into any of the jumps. Release your dog (I use *O.K.* as a release) and move slowly into the sequence.

At first, reward every turn your dog offers. When practicing circles it is important to move slowly yet remain slightly ahead of the dog. Remember you are leading, showing the way. You know the path but your dog does not. If you are clear about what you are doing with your body language, your dog can easily read your signals.

Practice this circle sequence with the dog on the outside, on both your right and left sides. Begin to observe which side seems more natural for your dog. With this in mind, train to your dog's weakness by spending more time on the weaker side. Agility is a two-sided sport. You and your dog should be ambidextrous.

Remember when we practiced large circles with the dog on the inside? The exercise in Figure C lends itself to practicing that skill. You will travel the larger circle and the dog the smaller one. This is also a good sequence for practicing rotation of the dog's hindquarters that you learned in Chapter 3. Remember to square off your shoulders as you turn toward each jump. That body signal gives needed information to your dog. Practice slowly at first, even at a walk. At first increase your rate of reinforcement by rewarding every turn that your dog offers. Give your dog the information he needs at this step.

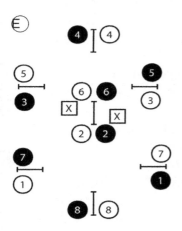

Crosses and Lead Changes

Many handlers use **Exercise E** for practicing and training front and rear crosses. Here again I suggest you split the sequence and practice jumps #1 through #3 black and white numbers as well as #5 through #7 since these are the points where the crossing turn should occur. The handler's approximate position for the front cross (Jumps #1 through #3) is indicated by the Xs on Figure E, in each case before the #2 jump. If you want more information on this sequence, see the article, "Agility Basics for Canines and Competitors: Walking the Course, Part 2," by Kathy Keats in the February 2005 issue of *Clean Run* magazine.

When starting this exercise it is crucial to practice your turns without your dog and practice the front-cross sections independent of the rest of the sequence until you are quite comfortable. You'll want to come back to this sequence time and time again as your handling improves. Down the road you'll add earlier and earlier cues. But for now as the dog lands off the second jump, step into the first step of your front cross. Complete the cross as shown at FC in **Figure F**. I ask my students to practice this step several times, all the while keeping their eye on their virtual dog. If you can perform the front cross without looking directly at the jump to your right (#2) but keeping it in your peripheral vision, you are ready to add your dog.

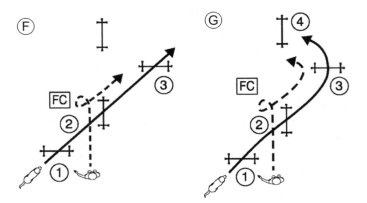

When adding your dog, at first practice only the three jumps for the front cross. Practice until you see your dog travel a straight line from jump #2 to jump #3. That straight line will tell you that he recognizes where you are going and he can turn earlier off jump #1. Many times you will see handlers ask the dog to make a 90° turn from one jump to another because they are late with their front-cross cues. Every step the dog takes in an unnecessary direction adds extra time on course. This exercise helps the dog and the handler run more efficiently.

When you have a good understanding of the front cross add additional jumps in the sequence until you can smoothly run the entire sequence. That means, for instance, you will have to alter your dog's path over jump #3 to make the turn to jump #4 as in **Figure G**. Be sure to practice in both directions.

This sequence can also be performed with rear crosses cued on the take-off side of jumps #3 and #6, but cross and reward on the landing side. Doing so will put you in a good position both to reinforce your dog and also to handle the upcoming #4 or #7 jump, respectively. Remember, practice your footwork and hand signals in this sequence before adding your dog.

Some Final Thoughts

Flatwork is something that should be part of every dog's initial training. Many handlers continue working elements of flatwork as part of their dog's agility training for life. Since flatwork is simply agility handling and movement without the distraction of jumps and other obstacles, it is a valuable tool to keep in your training bag.

Today courses are becoming more difficult and intricate even at the Novice level. When I began running my first dog in AKC Novice, the courses were simple, straight-line affairs with a few turns and changes of lead. Weaves weren't even introduced until Open, so the knowledge and training leap from

Novice to Open was huge. It appears to me now that AKC Novice courses require a higher level of training than ever before and more closely resemble the old Open courses. Open courses are closer to what once were Excellent courses. And more sophisticated handling challenges are appearing in the lowest levels of other agility venues as well. The demands on a handler and dog increase each year. The use of flatwork enables the handler to work out and perfect handling before taking on the actual course elements. As a team you are able to define the cues and movements you will need and reinforce your dog for the appropriate understanding and response.

Used effectively, therefore, flatwork becomes a tool you need throughout your agility career. I hope the exercises and skills I've described in this book become only the first chapter in your development as an agility handler. As you continue in agility with your dog(s), I hope you can use these exercises as a jumping-off point to create your own toolbox of agility skills. So have fun, and may your teamwork flourish in the process.

Suggested Reading

Getting Started: Clicker Training for Dogs, Karen Pryor (2005) Sunshine Books

In FOCUS: Developing a Working Relationship with Your Performance Dog, Deborah Jones, Ph.D., and Judy Keller (2004) Clean Run Productions, LLC

Excelling at Dog Agility, Book 1: Obstacle Training, Jane Simmons-Moake (1999) FlashPaws Productions

Don't Shoot the Dog! The New Art of Teaching and Training, Karen Pryor (1999) Bantam Books

Excel–erated Learning, Explaining how dogs learn and how best to teach them, Pamela J. Reid, Ph.D. (1996) James and Kenneth Publishers

Smart Trainers: Brilliant Dogs, Janet Lewis (1997) Canine Sports Productions

"Baby Steps: Jump Foundation Exercises for Training Your Puppy," by Susan Garrett, *Clean Run*, Vol. 9, No. 3, March 2003

"Shape Up Your Training Program, Introduction to Shaping," by Deborah Jones, Ph.D., *Clean Run*, Vol. 12, No. 2, February 2006

"Agility Basics for Canines and Competitors: Walking the Course, Part 2," by Kathy Keats, *Clean Run*, Vol. 11, No. 2, February 2005

Dogwise.com is your source for quality books, ebooks, DVDs, training tools and treats.

We've been selling to the dog fancier for more than 25 years and we carefully screen our products for quality information, safety, durability and FUN! You'll find something for every level of dog enthusiast on our website dogwise.com or drop by our store in Wenatchee, Washington.

Made in the USA
Coppell, TX
09 April 2021

53403283R00044